BOARDROOM VERITIES

A celebration of trusteeship with
some guides and techniques
to govern by

Jerold Panas

Precept Press, Inc., Chicago

95   94   93   92   91   5   4   3   2   1

Library of Congress Catalog Card Number: 91-66145

International Standard Book Number: 0-944496-26-1

Precept Press, Inc.
160 East Illinois Street
Chicago, Illinois 60611

Composition by Point West Inc., Carol Stream, IL

Printed in the United States of America

Contents

"BUDGETS, BUILDINGS, AND BALONEY." WHAT A GREAT TIME TO BE A TRUSTEE!

DIFFICULT TIMES, THESE. Running a hospital is complex and confounding. Being president of a college can feel like walking a tightrope without a safety net. Heading a social agency requires the fortitude and faith of a Job.

It's an unscrutable fate, working at an institution. Any executive desiring a tranquil and unruffled life has done badly being born in the twentieth century.

The past looks better all the time. The future isn't what it used to be.

For a board member of an institution, it's not easy either. The legal liabilities, new regulations, and fiduciary responsibilities never end. And there are concerns about staff. All those objectives that were not reached. Deadlines that aren't met. Meetings, meetings, meetings. And enough red tape and tangle to make even a Houdini cower.

Too much to read. But not enough information. How can you make an informed decision?

As one college trustee told me recently, "All we talk about at board meetings are the three Bs—budgets, buildings, and baloney!"

Worst of all, always the talk about fundraising. Always. It never ends. Some say it's true, the story about the college president who wrote: "Send money now. I'll explain later."

But raising funds seems to get harder, no matter how aggressively you work at it. You have to run faster and faster just to stay in the race. Except now, the track is more slippery and steep.

And trustees are always being asked for money. It seems to be the favored hymn most often sung in every organization's repertoire. The first stanza refers to the responsibility of a trustee, with the old refrain: "It starts with the board, if trustees don't care and give, why should anyone else?"

It probably won't change. And I doubt that it will get better. I see a great future for more of the same!

But, ah—what magnificent things are happening in your organization. And you, you're a trustee. You make them happen.

Your organization is involved every day in saving a delinquent kid from a life on the street. Your hospitals saves lives every hour of every day. Your school makes scholarships available to young people who couldn't otherwise attend. Your institution is working on the cure for a disease—and they've almost found it.

It's magnificent. Glorious. Exhilarating. You're a trustee, and you make it happen.

You know it's worth it. You know it's paying off. Those long hours, the extra gift, the one-more committee meeting, the never-ending paper shuffle—but that's what it takes. The endless chicken dinners and the overcooked zucchini—you can even put up with that. You know that what you do affects the lives of hundreds and thousands, for generations to come.

The happy army of directors and trustees. There must be at least 15 million men and women in the country just like you. Giving selflessly of time and money to inspiring causes and great institutions. Your organization is winning battles of consequence every day. Saving lives and changing lives.

Blessed are the trustees, say I. In heaven you will surely stand on the right hand of the saints and martyrs!

But there are times you feel like Sisyphus, rolling that huge ball up a very high hill. The ball gets larger. The hill gets steeper. But you never stop, because you know it's worth it.

Lucky you. You are giving a part of your life to an organization that makes a difference of significant proportions. And they couldn't do it without you, and the other 15 million Americans just like you.

Read on. I am going to offer eighty Trustee Verities. Some may make the hill a little less steep, the ball a little lighter.

It still won't be easy. Whoever said that being a trustee was easy!

1

KEEP RAISING
THE BAR

YOU ARE A TRUSTEE. You are unwilling to settle for less than the very best and the highest quality in all that the organization does. And you encourage all board members to exercise the same demanding test. You keep raising the bar.

You provide whatever commitment of time is necessary. Your decisions demonstrate extraordinary judgment, not unlike Solomon. And you are dedicated to be sacrificial in your philanthropy.

You see, it's not at all complicated, this business of being a trustee. You understand the mission of the organization and you make certain that it is committed in writing in a way that can be understood by even a sixth grader. You see to it that all programs follow a rigorous pursuit of this philosophy.

You make certain the chief executive is the finest person possible for the job, and you give him or her the greatest

4

support in every manner possible. (You're even allowed to consider compensation rewards!) And if you have good staff, you get out of its way.

That's how easy it is to exercise good trusteeship.

Oh, and one more thing. You give it your heart and soul.

George Behrakis is the chief executive officer of Muro— one of the major pharmaceutical houses in the country. He is a hands-on manager, putting in long days, even on the weekends. For his business, he travels 60 percent of the time. Yet he still manages to be Chair of the board of St. John's Medical Center in Lowell, Massachusetts. He provides this extraordinary institution with unlimited energy, business acumen, and leadership. And a great deal of money, also.

Behrakis says: "If I'm going to do something, I give it my entire heart and soul. Why get into something if you're not going to give it everything you have? I don't care much for board members who sit on the sidelines and watch."

2

AT LEAST TWO OUT OF THREE

D R. HENRY W. WRISTON became president of Brown University in 1937. He served that post with great distinction for eighteen years. Before Wriston, Brown was a very fine school, but of no major national distinction. It was Wriston who developed it into what it is today—one of the elite universities in the nation.

How did he do this? Through sheer force of vision and leadership. Plus an outstanding board of trustees. He did it because he had the funding that was necessary—to transform a carbon copy school into one of the greatest universities in the country.

"Soon after I went to Brown," Wriston said, "someone asked me to tell them what I expected from a trustee. They asked me to be quite explicit, right to the point. I didn't need much time to think about it. My response was 'Work, Wealth, and Wisdom. Preferably, I want all three, but if I must I would settle for a minimum of two out of the three.' "

That formula has stood the test of time.

Work, Wealth, Wisdom. You can have a very sophisticated and complex system for rating potential trustees, but nothing provides a more cogent assessment than "The Three Ws."

You want trustees who are willing to work, willing to give the time necessary to attend committee meetings, review financial statements, and endure the overly long reports.

And of course, you want trustees who are wise. You want men and women who can bring mature judgment to very complex matters. At times, the decisions you face at a board meeting are much like Churchill's quip about Russia: A puzzle, inside a riddle, wrapped in an enigma. You need the best minds possible, wise enough to make the right decision within a very short timeframe.

And wealth! Ah! You need those who are willing to make sacrificial gifts. Men and women who can make or influence large gifts. Give or Get!

So measure an incoming slate carefully. If you have a candidate with all three Ws, you have a prime selection. That's a person who brings a lot to the party. If you have a person who brings two of the three Ws, you still have a viable selection. But only one W? Better to keep the vacancy open for the right person.

You can afford to have a vacancy. Keep working at this until you have precisely the right person. What your organization cannot afford is a one W trustee.

3

WHEN TO PASS

"I 'D GO ON TO the next one. That's what I'd do." That is C. Allen Favrot speaking.

Allen knows what he's talking about. I'll explain in a moment. But first read these credentials. He has been Chair and Chief Volunteer Officer of the United Way in New Orleans, and Chair of the board of directors of the Young Men's Christian Association. He has headed both the capital campaign for the YMCA and the United Way. He is past Chair of the board of the Blue Ridge Assembly, a national training center. He has headed a dozen more organizations. He is a recipient of every major award his native city of New Orleans can bestow on an honored son.

I asked Allen what his reaction would be if he spoke to a person about serving on one of his boards and the man or woman said: "I'll join the board, but you can't count on me for a gift and I won't call on anyone."

"Allen," I asked, "what would you do?"

"I'd go on to the next one. I wouldn't consider adding someone to our board who isn't interested enough to make a gift or to call on others. I don't care how well known he is in the community or what his name might mean to the organization, it would be obvious that he doesn't bring the kind of commitment that is necessary. I'd pass him by and go on to the next one.

"I remember your telling me, Jerry, that a board member should: give, get, or get-off. I really practice that."

Allen feels that the amount isn't what is significant. "Some board members may not be able to give a large amount. That's okay. But there must be something. Every board member can do something."

"And, or course, I would expect them to call on others for gifts.

"There's no room in the typical organization for names on the letterhead. There might have been a time in the past when you could say to someone: 'Just let me use your name, that will be enough.' But those days are gone. Everybody's involvement counts.

"If you don't get someone who is willing to work and give, you are settling for less than the best. And I don't think any organization can afford that these days."

Recently, I had occasion to talk with a member of the advisory board of The Salvation Army in New York City. I asked him to tell me honestly why he serves on the board. It isn't even a policy-making group—it is indeed only advisory in scope and nature.

"Before I answer that," he said: "Let me tell you what it costs me. First of all, it's the two or three hours at each board meeting. I attend six or eight of those a year. And then there are the other functions that I attend as a matter of regular routine. It's those hours of my life that nobody could possibly pay me for—that's what it costs me. And then I send them four or five thousand dollars a year, sometimes a little bit more when they really need it. And then, of course, it's the tickets and the tables that you buy for special events. But mostly, it's my time, and there is absolutely no way anyone could repay me for that.

"Now, I'll tell you why I do it. I don't need another board, and I don't need any more recognition."

"I think of what The Salvation Army does. I think of all of the pregnant teenagers they take care of. And the battered women. And the homeless. Those people wouldn't have anywhere else to go if it weren't for The Salvation Army. They take these guys off the street, feed them, and try to dry them out.

"I honestly believe, in my heart of hearts, that by serving on the board of The Army, I am saving the lives of hundreds and hundreds of men and women. That's why I do it. I really believe I am making a contribution. In my own small way, I'm making a difference in my part of the world. I don't do that in my corporate life and I don't do that in my church. But in my board activity with The Salvation Army, I really make a difference.

"When I measure the contribution I make to the lives of others, those few hours I spend and the few dollars—they melt away. In fact, just thinking about it and talking with you about it makes me feel that I should be doing a heck of a lot more."

And that's it—a million others just like this Salvation Army board member, and just like you. In your own special way, you are changing a corner of the world.

4

MISSION IS EVERYTHING

A POSITIVE REPUTATION FROM past victories often can cover up a fading institution. But not forever. Sooner or later, you will be known for what you are, not what you were.

A momentous breakthrough happens, says John W. Gardner, when an institution responds with vigor and relevance to the needs of its day, when its morale and vitality are high, when it holds itself to unsparing standards of performance.

Breaking old barriers. Crossing new thresholds. Reaching new horizons. It all starts with the board. It takes a team of dedicated men and women who share a common vision and are willing to pursue the dream with passion and vigor.

An attachment to time honored ways can become an anchor. Reverence for heritage and roots can act like barnacles. A mission needs to welcome change.

An organization requires a searing, soul-searching self-analysis. Not once in a while. On a regular basis. But this kind of rigorous, piercing assessment can be frightening because it may expose the most sacred programs and activities as being ineffectual. It may uncover someone's pet project as being void of mission. But without the assessment, an organization can become blind to its defects, insensitive in its service, fall short in its outreach.

Some boards have an unwritten law: Don't bother us. We won't change. We stand firm on stagnation.

Boards must have a reviewing and renewing process that can provide for objective observation and captious criticism. The some-time dissenter and the trustee who doesn't always conform must be heard and understood. A challenge of the status quo should not be merely tolerated, it should be welcomed and encouraged. A crank can be a troublemaker. But a crank also ignites an engine.

You have seen it happen. The moment comes at a board meeting for a decision. There appears to be approval. And there he goes again asking all those questions and delaying action. He starts by saying: "I hate to be the devil's advocate, but. . ." And you know that the "but" is the launching of a tedious discourse. You pray that he doesn't start with the founding of the institution and work his way through each of the 87 years of the organization. The meeting will never end. It is a fragile moment. But, the board must protect the trustee who is a critic. You must even protect the trustee who is a bore!

The effective board is concerned less about how things are done. It is greatly concerned about why things are done. A thoughtful trustee looks with appreciation and never-ending delight at expanding services, larger numbers, and a bigger budget. But he keeps his eye forever on the mission of the institution. It is the implacable and profound purpose of the organization that assures its success.

The mission is an organization's most prized treasure—to be taken out often for public display, to be cherished, and to be polished regularly to make certain it maintains its luster and value.

You can reach new levels of achievement without serving your mission. But you will atrophy or finally die. Even if you are very active, you will become immobilized. Your mission will be strangled by a tangle of programs and activities without purpose.

Your mission must not be a recital of where you have been. It speaks eloquently as to where you are going.

5

MONEY MAKES
IT HAPPEN

IN THIS VOLUME'S BIBLIOGRAPHY (page 227), I have
listed forty-two books which relate to boards and trusteeship. They are all excellent. If I didn't feel they were worthy of reading, I would not have included them.

Chief among these is "Governing Boards" by Cyril O.
Houle. It is comprehensive, insightful, and the work of one
who knows his field. Every Chair and every chief executive
officer should consider it required reading.

What I found fascinating, however, is what was left out.

There was not one reference to philanthropy, to giving,
or the responsibility of board members to secure the necessary funds to maintain the service and quality of their organization. To my way of thinking, the book provided the
body, but without the heart.

Money makes it happen. That's no guarantee, but it certainly helps. Proper funding, if appropriately used, can secure and sustain quality staff. It can buy necessary

equipment. It provides scholarships and camperships, food for the hungry, healthcare for those who need it, a bed for the homeless, and hope and hand for those who are without spirit or promise.

I call it "the extra margin." Your organization sustains its work and services from grants or the United Way. Or from program services and membership fees. Or some form of earned income. And importantly, from gifts. Even school districts that receive their funding from tax authorities have found that a private Foundation dedicated to the school, can provide consequential funds—"the extra margin."

As a trustee, you do indeed carry responsibility for "the extra margin." These are the funds that transform a so-so organization into a good one. A good one into a great one.

It is you, the trustee, who determines the success and future of your organization. You make it happen.

In many organizations, it does not take a large infusion of gifts to make a difference. Even a small amount can be of extraordinary consequence.

6

YOU MAKE A DIFFERENCE

"ALL I WANT TO do is change the world." That's Dr. Marianne McDonald speaking. It's the reason she serves as a trustee. And she serves on a number of boards. Where she finds the time is anyone's guess.

An extraordinary woman, Marianne McDonald. She has a black belt in karate and raises peacocks on her estate in Rancho Santa Fe, California. She is active in her church, her community, and in state politics.

She is a classicist and has an earned doctorate. The professor who supervised her thesis says she is very likely the most brilliant student who has ever graduated from the university. She has written three books and enough professional papers to fill four full pages of a curriculum vitae.

She can be daunting. Her conversation is filled with quotations from Euripides, Plato, and Socrates. It's a little hard to argue with that! She is fluent in Japanese and Greek, both ancient and modern. Of course. And she is a world-class skier and fencer. But there's not much time for that. She is active on several boards in Greece and is a visiting professor of Trinity College in Ireland.

She has seemingly unlimited energy. I introduced her once to a group as a combination of Auntie Mame and Joan of Arc. That's not far from the mark.

Well, how does she manage to do it all and still serve on six major boards of trustees—two that are international and one that is national? She says she manages because she finds the time.

"I believe in happiness. I believe in pursuing it and in following a philosophy that sustains it. And one of the things that gives me tremendous happiness in my life is serving on boards and helping others. I believe strongly that I have a responsibility to give back to my community. It drives me. I am convinced that by serving others you gain much more for yourself."

Marianne McDonald not only serves, she gives. She was recently named Philanthropist of the Year. She gives tremendous sums to a variety of organizations. "I try to avoid my accountant and business manager. I give away far too much—much more than I can take advantage of from a tax standpoint. But it's the giving that provides me the happiness."

As you can imagine, Dr. McDonald is asked to serve on many more boards than she can possibly accept. She tries to be selective and take on those where she has a particular interest or where she feels keenly she can help, save or change lives. After all, all she wants to do is change the world!

In the foreword of a recent book, David Rockefeller wrote: "...The nonprofits have been asked to take on some of the toughest challenges we face in sustaining both our global society and our individual communities." He says that in order to handle the responsibility effectively, trustees must be strong, dedicated, and courageous. And further, note this: "These boards must be informed and fearless in giving and seeking financial help to carry out their work."

It is an extraordinary phenomenon of this nation that there are millions of trustees, not unlike Marianne McDonald and David Rockefeller, who are unflagging in their devotion to serve their community, the nation, indeed the world, in a variety of wonderful causes.

And that's what makes your own involvement so special. As a trustee in your own organization, you know that you join millions of other leaders in a crusade to change the world.

Goethe said: "Whatever you can do, or dream you can do, begin it." Commitment is full of genius, power, and magic. All things become possible. Begin now.

7

SHARE THE LOAD

To be a good board member and discharge your responsibilities effectively obviously requires time and energy. If they told you differently when you were recruited, you now know better. But trusteeship can be great fun and there can be an immense sense of achievement. If the load is shared, the trip can be a wondrous journey.

There's the story of sharing that's as old as time. It's one of the earliest descriptions of board organization and teamwork. It's from the book of Exodus. It is an eloquent lesson in delegation and planning.

You may remember that Moses was everywhere, as busy as a person could possibly be, doing all kinds of things for his people. He wanted others to share the burden and he knew that this was the right thing to do, but a little bit of ego also was involved. Even a man of God can have a healthy ego. There was this business about the Tablets, speaking to Him direct, and having multitudes count on you. Well, that's all pretty heady stuff.

Moses had a son-in-law. Jethro. Regularly, Jethro spoke to Moses about how to deal with the serious problem of the increasing demand on Moses' time. Jethro, he was a bit like a management consultant!

One day, Moses sat as usual, listening to all the people's complaints against each other. This went on from early morning until way past dinner time.

When Moses came home late one evening, Jethro was waiting for him. "Why are you trying to do this all alone," said Jethro. "People are standing all day long in line, waiting to talk with you and get your help. You're going to wear yourself out—and if you do, what will happen to all the people? Moses, the job is too heavy a burden for you to handle all by yourself. Not only that, there are some awfully good folks around who are very capable—and when you're no longer here, someone will have to take your place.

"Now listen Moses, and let me give you a word of advice.

"Find some capable, godly, honest men and appoint them to work with you. We can get a few folks together and decide who ought to be involved. We want to enlist men who will work just as hard as you do and are just as concerned about the welfare of all of our people. Maybe some ought to have a treasure big enough so that if any of our people need alms or charity, they will be able to give what is necessary. You know, Moses, when you get people involved, they will be willing to do more and more for you.

"Get one dedicated man for each 1000 people. He in turn will have ten under him, each in charge of 100. And under each one of them will be two, each responsible for the affairs of 50. And each of these will have five beneath him, each taking care of ten persons. Let these men be responsible for all of the affairs, but anything that is too important or too complicated can still be brought to you. But the smaller matters, they can take care of themselves.

"Let one man be responsible for all of our funds. You will appoint him. Then we'll need another to be sure that we keep the Law. And one more to be sure that our property is in good keep. And still one more to be confident our services are meeting the needs. There should also be one more to be certain we are planning properly for the future.

If you do all of this, Moses, the way will be easier for you because you will share the burden with others. And in time, this will become a new and sacred law—The Delegation of Responsibility."

This is taken exactly from the book of Exodus, chapter 18, verses 13 through 22. Well, it is written very close to what I have reported. The lesson is that the responsibilities of trusteeship must be shared. If only a few do the work, the load is too heavy.

If the Chair doesn't delegate, or takes all of the credit, the board doesn't grow. Nor does the organization.

And if old-timers don't allow fresh, young blood to come in and take a full part, the organization may continue on—but it will surely die from lack of vitality and zeal.

8

THE CHAIR'S SPEED SETS THE PACE

T HE BOARD'S CHAIR DETERMINES and defines the character and style of the institution. The Chair provides, in a major way, the character and dimension and pace for the chief executive officer. The Chair guides, encourages, and supports the work of the entire enterprise in ways of consequential proportions.

In a significant way, he also develops and designs the profile of the board—how it acts and reacts, and how greatly it enjoys its myriad tasks. The Chair gives soul and spirit to the trustees. The Chair is your organization's chief executive volunteer, its driving force, the embodiment of all that is vital and effective about the organization. The Chair is your leader—and at times, the Cheer Leader.

The Chair must be willing to take the risk, the blame, the brunt, and the storm. And there always seems to be all of this in abundance!

For the Chair, there is a willingness to endure. A devotion to work. And most of all, a passion to win.

He brings other trustees along with him, at times laboriously and painstakingly. He extends new institutional frontiers with indomitable persistence.

The Chair is often a non-conformist, a dissenter, and a malcontent. But he understands fully that his job is to bring out opinions and feeling in others. He keeps his own peace, and makes peace among all.

Along with other trustees and staff, the Chair strives for the very best. He knows that the difference between failure and success is often the difference in doing something nearly right and doing it exactly right.

With the power to persuade and motivate others to heights believed unreachable, the Chair inspires, and is an inspiration.

The Chair has the heart and mind to work with trustees in making decisions quickly and decisively. And there is fierce faith, worthy of purpose and ideal. He speaks openly, plainly, and frankly. When he speaks, others listen. And act.

He is a barrier-breaking visionary. An opportunity seeker and seizer. For his organization, he does not easily suffer a second-place position. He understands that a good loser—is a loser. There is an exhilaration in winning, but always for the common good. He admonishes his trustees to not be do-gooders, but doers of good.

The Chair promotes a can-do spirit, uninhibited and unencumbered by the past. Great organizations, premier institutions, have been built on the drive and inspiration of just such leaders.

When the ancient Greek Aeschines spoke, the crowds said: "How well he speaks, what glorious words, what magnificent tones." But when Demosthenes spoke, they shouted: "Let us march against Philip. Now."

Let Aeschines speak his beautiful works. We are resoundly for Demosthenes. That is what great boards and elite organizations are built on.

9

ACCEPT BECAUSE YOU WANT TO SERVE

I CONDUCTED A SURVEY several years ago involving 6000 hospital trustees. I wanted to find out what prompts busy men and women to serve on a hospital board, an activity that takes an inordinate amount of time. They are forced to make bold decisions on matters that puzzle and perplex.

The response was clarion clear. They were on the board because it provided them an opportunity to serve their community and mankind. That was unquestionably the primary factor. There wasn't a close second.

Certainly, there are those who will serve because of the prestige, particularly if it is a distinguished institution. In fact, we found even those who want to serve mankind, don't mind the extra ego-massaging. But it's not the ego and it's not being able to add an extra listing in the Who's Who entry that motivates these people.

Saving lives and changing lives. The exhilaration of knowing that you are doing something that is helping others, that has meaning—that's what leaves an indelible mark. That's why people serve.

I read a little pamphlet recently for new attorneys. It was written to help them develop a new practice. It advised these young men and women to seek positions as quickly as possible on nonprofit boards. It's called casting one's net. "It's an excellent way to meet new people and build a practice." And indeed it is. But if they are worth anything at all, these young attorneys, that's not what captures them in the end. They become committed to their organization when they know that through their effort, they are truly making a difference in peoples' lives.

The opportunity to serve the community and mankind. That's pretty lofty stuff. But it's the stuff that great board members are made of. When your board is comprised of men and women with that ideal, totally dedicated to the mission of your institution—great things can happen.

Some people seek trusteeship to be something. Others accept the responsibility to do something. Avoid the former and cultivate the latter.

SIXTY QUESTIONS TO ANSWER

A RTHUR C. FRANTZREB IS one of today's great voices in the nonprofit field. When he speaks, you'd better listen! A college trustee once said to me: "When Art Frantzreb talks to our board, I want to chisel every word in stone."

Art has produced a magnificent 7-page booklet called *Non-Profit Organization Individual Governing Board Membership Audit*. That's a very long name for a really incomparable booklet costing only a few dollars. Every trustee should take the test, and every institution should order copies for its entire board. The address is in the bibliography section of this volume.

My own feeling is that the booklet should be the focus of a day and a half board retreat. Get off to somewhere quiet, undisturbed and unhurried, a place nice enough that you can do some creative freewheeling—and have a go at this booklet.

Here you will find important questions that will test your understanding of a trustee's responsibilities, your commitment, and your fervor. There's nothing else quite like it.

There are no right or wrong answers. Only real answers. Go somewhere and just spread out like molasses. Have a thorough discussion and make an assessment of each trustee's rating and an evaluation of the board as a whole.

Arthur Frantzreb says: "The board member's personal and professional talent, skill, experience, wisdom, judgment, and generous philanthropic support set the pace for both recognition and financial support of the organization as it continues to serve future generations. When you finish the audit, you'll know exactly what your role is and how effectively you meet the criteria of board membership. You'll uncover, also, how to get the greatest fulfillment and reward from your board service."

In the Appendix of this book, you will find an evaluation form which I designed for rating your board. It is quite different than any you have seen before. It is called TAB— *TRUSTEE ASSESSMENT of the BOARD.*

There are sixty specific characteristics and criteria for you to check and grade. The rating of your board can then be compared against some national norms.

TAB requires about fifteen minutes to complete. The scoring will take another five or ten. It's well worth the time. You will find the results fascinating—all that, and extremely helpful and productive, too. Best of all, use it with other trustees for a thorough discussion and analysis of your board's effectiveness.

TAB is no better than Arthur Frantzreb's superb grid, or any other of the fine board evaluations you have seen—but it is different. Whatever form you use, it should become the basis of individual introspection and the platform for a thoughtful, unhurried examination of small groups of trustees or the whole board.

As a trustee, you are morally and legally committed to provide proper stewardship. When you finish the evaluation and the discussions involved in responding to these questions, you will understand the immense joy of serving as a board member. You will understand, also, the responsibilities and trust which are yours. It is indeed a public trust. That is why I prefer the word *trustee*, rather than director—it implies a public faith in you as guardian, someone in whose care the welfare and growth of the organization has been entrusted. No modest responsibility, this.

11

BE PROUD
TO SERVE

THERE ARE TIMES THAT having an effective board is more than enlisting trustees with commitment, wisdom, and the ability to give generously. Sometimes, it's just plain sheer luck. Like getting safely across a busy street in Manhattan.

In a recent article, the *Harvard Business Review* reported: "To find a truly effective board, you are much better advised to look in the nonprofit sector than in our public corporations." You can check the July-August, 1989, issue of the *Review* for a full explanation.

Small wonder you leave some board meetings with a special glow of achievement. Chances are that even in the most trying and stressful of situations, your board makes consequential decisions, often with only a brief discussion and precious little time, and determines the destiny of the institution for years to come. And it all seems to work marvelously.

It's amazing, too, how far-reaching and insightful the strategic planning most often is and how effectively the staff and the trustees combine a shared responsibility—and end up with a monumentally successful design.

Someone asked recently what a large Catholic hospital chain and a successful Japanese company had in common. The answer was that the hospital chain's credo for all staff and board members was: "If it's in the patient's interest, we have to promote it as effectively as we can. Then, it's our job to make it pay." That's how the Japanese do it, also. They start with the mission, then, they go to the next step—to make it happen in the marketplace. The rewards follow.

That's the answer. You start with the mission, and you end with the mission. You must regard the mission of your institution as the Baptist preacher accepts the New Testament—with unyielding and unbending faith!

Outside our own country, there is nowhere in the world that has quite the type of board structure or performance we do.

Take the American Red Cross, for instance—the largest non-governmental agency in the world. It is, also, probably one of the most complex. It operates thousands of blood banks, skin banks, and bone banks. And handles worldwide disaster relief. And provides first-aid courses in thousands of schools. And yet, it did not have its first professional chief executive officer until 1950. The work was handled by board members.

The Girl Scouts have nearly a million volunteers and board members—and only a few thousand paid professionals. It's a marvel to have all those men and women working in your behalf, and head over heels in love with the cause and the work. Peter Drucker says the Girl Scouts is the best managed corporation in the world—and that includes major businesses as well an nonprofits.

You are a board member and you can make an everlasting difference for your institution and the public you serve. It's an awesome responsibility, at times not without agony and pain. But it is also one of the most fulfilling and satisfying jobs you can undertake.

For some, it is the balance in their life. H.I. Romnes, former President and Chief Executive Officer of AT&T, told me that the several board responsibilities he carried helped round out his life. "I love my work, and I'm devoted to it day and night. But I wouldn't give up the couple agency boards I serve on for anything."

12

WHO TO KEEP

YOU'RE NOT GOING TO like this but chances are that sometime soon you may be getting a Report Card on your performance as a board member. If you don't, you should.

An increasing number of organizations spend a great deal of time evaluating their trustees. To maintain the viability and vitality of an organization, trustees should be assessed once a year by their peers.

I can almost hear some of you saying: "You've got to be crazy. We're having a tough enough time right now recruiting board members. If they think that they're going to be graded, we won't get anyone!"

I am convinced that there are busy men and women who are waiting to be asked, waiting to join in your work and share in your significant cause. I feel just as certain that the more stringent and demanding your requirements, the more likely you are to enlist and maintain the kind of trustees who can make a difference to the organization. The evidence indicates I'm right on this issue.

I like the idea of having a standing committee of the board that carries the charge for evaluating board members. You can call it what you wish or whatever seems appropriate, but my favorite name for this kind of group is: The Committee on Trusteeship. That seems to say it all. It should meet once a month and in addition to an on-going evaluation of individual trustees, it should be responsible for nominating new board members. If a group like that meets once a month and really work at it, you are certain to enlist the strongest board possible.

The Committee on Trusteeship needs to take an analytical, objective look regularly at your present trustees to determine what they bring to the board table. This means the age mix, social strata, and the financial resources they bring to the party. The Committee must determine how trustees are to be selected and evaluated, and how performance might be strengthened.

You should remove non-performers and non-attenders from the board. What good are they? Or move them over to an honorary group, if necessary.

I understand full well the importance of keeping a major donor or holding on to someone who shows signs of making a large gift. The Committee on Trusteeship can be effective in moving people where their talents fit the best, or in counseling them to leave the board and return when they have more time. That's tough. But that is also what makes a taught, loyal, and hardworking group with high flying esprit.

The YMCA in Nashville, Tennessee, establishes objectives each year for their board members and volunteers. Then, an evaluation is made against these goals. If they don't meet their objectives, they are asked to resign or they are re-assigned to some other responsibility. They must have a terrible time recruiting? Wrong! They have an elite board, probably one of the very strongest in the area.

Board members will keep surprising you. They'll stand on tiptoes for the right organization, and take on assignments that were once thought to be impossible. Make them stretch. They will.

13

GIVE, GET, OR GET OFF

WELL, YOU'VE HEARD THIS one—"When they asked me to come on the board, they told me I wouldn't have to give." Or how about: "I was told that I wouldn't have to ask anyone for money."

And there are trustees who believe: "I give my time and therefore I shouldn't be expected to give any money."

But that's naive, to think that your time alone will provide the resources necessary to thrust the institution forward.

The admonition: "Give, Get, or Get off" makes a great deal of sense. Particularly in today's world. Fortunate is the organization that has trustees who are willing to give their time and energy. But whatever is in their capacity to give, they should provide financial resources, also. Every trustee should be expected to give something.

Herbert K. Cummings is a philanthropist of note. He and his wife support an array of important activities in

Phoenix. He was recently named Philanthropist of the Year, but he could just as easily have received the citation for Volunteer of the Year.

For those activities he supports, he provides his talents and funds in extraordinary proportions. He says: "I serve on a number of boards and have been the Chair of more than my share. I can tell you that when I ask others to serve on a board with me, I make it quite clear that they are expected to work and to give. I ask them to match my giving—not necessarily in the amount but in proportion and in devotion. I'm not really so interested in the amount they give, but I think it is important that whatever it is, it should represent a significant gift for them. I can't imagine anyone taking the responsibility of a board membership and not recognizing that this involves giving on their part. The amount is important. Their participation is even more so.

"As for myself, I couldn't possibly imagine being asked to serve on a board without an understanding that there is a financial commitment involved—implied or otherwise. And that probably means if I am not willing to make that kind of a commitment, I shouldn't accept. If you know, for instance, that the organization is about ready to take on a capital campaign and they ask you to serve on the board— well, you just know that means you're going to be asked for a gift. If you feel good about the organization, I think you ought to take it on.

"It's a privilege to serve on a board. But if you don't feel good enough about the group to make a gift, for heaven's sake, don't take it on. Do something else like tend to your garden or read a good book."

14

EIGHT EASY RESPONSIBILITIES

TWO ITEMS OF TRUSTEE accountability probably dominate all others. The first is that the board has the final
responsibility for determining the institution's mission and
its objectives. It should examine this on a regular basis.
The board establishes the tone and character for the institution and its philosophy of operation. It is one of the ines-
capable functions of the board and you as a trustee.

Secondly, it's your job to select the chief executive officer.
No easy task this. If you've got a good executive, hold on for
all your might. Choke him or her with gold if necessary! If
the executive is only ho-hum or less than that, it is your responsibility to do something about it. If you don't, you are
not discharging your trustee responsibilities properly and you
are inhibiting the pace and success of the institution.

It's your job to evaluate the chief executive officer on a
regular basis, and provide appropriate compensation. If
you have a particularly good person, by the way, there's no

harm in having the highest paid in their classification. If they're really good, why not? Someone has to be the highest.

The board has the responsibility for establishing short-term objectives and long-range goals. You need to work at this all the time and plan as creatively and strategically as possible.

Some would put this next item nearly at the top of the list. You have to make certain that your organization has the necessary financial resources to meet its mission. And to provide a program of bounding vitality, broad scope, and high quality. Money helps make this all happen.

Board members sometimes shy away from planning and priority-setting. They may not even wish to become involved in mission statements and philosophy.

But one fact of life that every board member must accept is the need to provide proper funding. Give or get. Preferably both!

And obviously, you have to manage the institution's resources with great care and effectiveness. Being a good member means being a good steward.

There are other things, of course—like making certain the organization maintains quality programs and services and understands how to market. And trustees have a responsibility for being advocates for the institution—they mustn't miss an opportunity to sing its praise.

If you have done all these things, there is but one thing more. Stay out of the way! Your job is not to manage. It is to determine policy. When you take on the staff's role, it is a certain sign that you do not understand fully your responsibilities or—you have the wrong staff. If it is the latter, go back to rule number two, and start all over!

See how easy it all is. As Mark Twain said about Wagner's music: "It's not as bad as it sounds."

15

MAKE TIME

JUST ABOUT EVERYONE FEELS the time-crunch and stress. Research shows that particularly among middle and high income individuals, there is more and more of a desire for leisure time—and less and less time to enjoy it. But those who give their time and talent to nonprofits, they seem to feel the glow and joy of serving on a board. These folks, they're busy, also. They don't have time. But they make it. Nothing seems to take the place of the inner-satisfaction and rewards they feel.

Take J. Peter Grace, Jr., for instance. He runs a $6 billion corporation. Some say he runs it single-handedly. The company operations comprise more than 2700 facilities in all the states, and also in 45 countries around the world.

Mr. Grace is now in his mid-70s and still going strong. Apparently, stronger than ever. You hear about people who start slowly—and then taper off! Not Peter Grace. He still puts in a 90-hour week. You read it correctly: ninety hours!

And thirty hours of that is his involvement and work for charities.

He says: "You're born to serve the Lord and the brotherhood of man...and I think everybody's obligation is to help...so, if that's right—and I think it's right—then you've got to work your ass off everyday to do that." Perhaps not eloquent, but you certainly know where he stands.

He's the same, whether it is in his executive office or at the board meeting at St. Vincent's Medical Center where he serves as a trustee. "Some say I'm a slave driver. If it is slave driving, then I'm a slave, too, because I never ask anybody to do anything that I wouldn't do or don't do myself. When I'm interested in something, I give it everything. And I get totally lost in the project."

He has served on the board of Fordham University and a host of other major Catholic institutions. Why does he do this? What drives him?

One part of it is that he feels he can transfer some of his abundant management talents to the nonprofit sector. And any staff executive of an institution where Grace serves on the board better have their details and numbers in order. He is a number machine.

But that's not the real reason he serves and gives his time. What is indeed important to the extraordinary Peter Grace is the opportunity he sees in every trusteeship to serve mankind. On this point, he is deadly serious. And there's an interesting ego factor in all this. It's not the need for name recognition. He's had plenty of that. But one thing that does seem to feed his ego is the glow and satisfaction he feels in knowing that those institutions he serves provide an array of services that are very special and of immense consequence.

Grace knows that as a trustee, he helps make this happen. You make it happen, too, by your good grace.

16

KEEP YOUR MISSION SIMPLE

THE MISSION OF YOUR organization describes the philosophy and focus of your operation. It places you without parallel. It is the platform from which you launch your service program with heart and spirit. The mission statement is not sloganism—it is the life of your organization.

As a trustee, you with other members of the board, are responsible for having a statement of your mission which is relevant and timely. It is an enabling and empowering statement—the engine which propels your institutional train. It resonates with the unique combination of your ethos, rationale, and philosophy.

As a board member, you understand the mission. You understand that in today's world, you either carve out your niche—or you'll be niched! You never lose sight of your organization's unique culture and character.

The mission statement has to be understandable. If a

grade schooler can read, comprehend, and explain the statement, you are probably on the right track. You have performed well as a trustee!

To understand the mission is critical, because it is the overriding criterion by which you measure the success of your programs and activities, your marketing plan, and your funding structure.

You are the guardian and protector of your organization's mission—and at the same time you must be willing to set it free. In order to be effective, you must know your institution's heritage, what is considered the greatest and the brightest—and then feel totally unencumbered and disassociated with the past and status quo. You understand that these are new days and new times, and this requires new thinking and perhaps a new focus. What is important is: Where are you going. Not, where have you been.

Once the mission is approved, it becomes your organization's credo, the hymn you continually sing—with gusto, conviction, and zeal.

17

DO YOUR THING

MARTHA INGRAM IS SINGLE-MINDED and driven. Wondrously so. She is an achiever and not easily satisfied until a job has been done, and done properly.

She is a member of the board of directors and heads the Public Affairs division of Ingram Industries—reported to be one of the largest privately held company in the nation. She is devoted, some would say obsessed!—with seeing to it that Nashville has the finest array of activities in all disciplines of the arts. In Nashville, when it comes to the arts, nothing escapes Martha Ingram's fine touch, volunteer leadership, and philanthropy.

As far as awards or recognition is concerned, she has had it all. But that's not what motivates her. She feels that people come to Nashville and expect certain amenities, and the city has to grow culturally as well as corporately. She puts her dedication into action—both in terms of her financial and her leadership support. In Nashville, she's in the forefront of everything good that has to do with culture and the arts. There isn't a single advance in recent years which she has not spearheaded.

"I think I am interested in the arts because you get to see the end product so quickly. There's a symphony performance or there is a painting, or a dance. And there you have it. You have helped raise the money to make it happen and you get to see or hear the final product right away. It is very exciting."

The Ingrams, Martha and her husband Bronson, are considered Nashville's leading philanthropists. But she's an indefatigable worker, also. One community leader told me: "When Martha makes an appointment to see me, I know I'm in trouble! I know it's going to cost a lot of money. But she's hard to resist or refuse. You know she puts her own money up first, and plenty of it."

There is a major lesson here. Those who both give and work, unquestionably provide the greatest strength to an organization. When you bring both qualities to your trusteeship, there is a synergism that takes place—a clear case of one plus one equals three. A person who is asked for a gift from a trustee like Martha Ingram knows that the board member has put their commitment where their purse is.

There's another lesson. Trustees can only do their most effective best and give to the fullest extent, both their leadership and dollars—to those organizations where they have deep conviction. Martha Ingram says: "I don't get on boards of organizations that are heavily involved with social action. I know how important this is, but it simply isn't my thing. I feel that people ought to get head-over-heels involved with those things that are important to them." And there it is. Trustees provide the greatest contribution possible when there is a love affair with their organization.

That's it. Passion. A trustee with passion is a majority.

Passion is the difference between flapping your wings and flying.

And there is one last lesson. Perhaps the greatest. Very likely the most generous gift of all is the trustee who serves, and serves faithfully.

Martha Ingram speaks eloquently on that point. "I get upset—I get more than a little upset—with people who don't get completely involved and become totally identified with the organization. They may come to you with only a low level of dedication. That's perhaps to be expected. But you always hope that growth will take place and they will become enthralled with the organization. I think it should be something close to a love affair. My father told me something that made a great impression on me. He said: 'When you pass through life, make certain that somehow the world is a little better place because you passed through it.' Every time I attend a meeting, I think about that and I really try to make the world a little better place. That's what keeps me going."

18

THE BALANCED BUDGET

NEXT TO GETTING AN unexpected tax refund or being shot at and missed—there's nothing quite as satisfying as a balanced budget.

There are two ways of looking at a balanced budget. The first is to cut expenses to meet income. This may appear to be the most obvious solution, but for some reason organizations that take this tact don't seem to do quite as well. They tend to fall behind their competition, their services become dull and ho-hum, quality suffers. The parade passes them by.

On the other hand, there is the organization that raises income to meet expenses. Easier said than done, this kind of thinking. But it makes for a vital, enterprising, and entrepreneurial institution.

It also requires a board that has faith and fervor, dedication and devotion. It will certainly mean that trustees will have to give more and almost certainly become more involved in calling on others to give.

No casual decision, this second alternative. But what an exciting difference it makes in the life and the service of your organization.

The financial statement doesn't tell the story. Hardly! The bottom line of your institution cannot be counted in dollars and cents. The true net worth can only be measured in how you affect the lives of those you serve. Changed lives and saved lives. For your organization, that's the only bottom line that really counts.

19

KEEP 'EM BUSY

I AM A GREAT believer in regular board and committee meetings. I am convinced that the more you involve people, the greater their dedication.

All the research I've done supports this. The more you bring people into the institutional loop, the greater their ownership. And the greater their ownership, the stronger their sense of commitment.

Organizations are faulted most often because trustees feel that the communication process is not very effective. "I just don't know what's going on." I hear that all the time. You can't even presume that because trustees attend every meeting and receive the minutes, they are getting the full message. I have had too many situations where that kind of an assumption turns out to be a leap of unwarranted faith.

I am, by the way, an enthusiastic advocate of having non-board members serve on major committees. This provides an extraordinary opportunity to develop a feeder system for the major league board. It also means that you can bring very special talent to a particular committee that might not serve the organization most effectively as a trustee. You will be able to enlist some remarkable marketing and PR talent for the Public Relations Committee, some who might not be particularly good for the governing board. The same would be true for the Finance Committee, the Investment Committee, the Program Committee, and the Property Committee.

I believe emphatically that every board meeting and committee session has to be painstakingly choreographed. This requires considerable thought and careful design. The staff plays an important part in working with the Chair in developing the agenda. This means setting aside ample time for the Chair and the chief staff officer prior to the meeting to assure a successful session.

Often, I have seen a Chair walk into a meeting completely unprepared. He looks at his agenda for the first time. But perhaps there isn't even a written agenda that's been prepared. I cringe! The meeting is a disaster.

Board meetings should provide for the unleashing of positive forces that carry the institution to new levels of impact, outreach, and service. The agenda should be planned and designed in such a way that there are decisions to be made and that trustees have a sense that the time they spent was worth the effort. I had a boss once who said: "Make certain that at every session, no matter whether it is a board or committee meeting—the group has a major decision to discuss and vote on." If you follow that dictum, you are certain to have effective and worthwhile sessions. Every meeting, a major discussion and decision.

Regular meetings are important because they provide a sense of ownership. They make the communication process easier. If they are planned and orchestrated properly, meetings can bring trustees a great sense of achievement.

20

NEVER TOO OLD

WINTON M. BLOUNT IS the most highly esteemed trustee in the nation. That's the award he won in 1991—the Distinguished Service Award, given to the person in the country who has demonstrated extraordinary leadership and dedication in serving their institutions of higher education. That's long overdue, that honor for Blount.

I doubt that anyone has ever called him Winton, except perhaps for his mother. He is known as Red by everyone. "I love it when someone calls me Red. It reminds me of those days, long ago, when I had enough hair that someone could tell what color it was!"

Blount has served as trustee of the University of Alabama for three decades. His list of achievements during that time would fill a book—but most prominent, very likely, was his strong and total opposition to Governor George Wallace's "I'll stand in the schoolhouse door" on the eve of the university's enrollment of two black students. That was in 1963. And Red Blount has been taking a strong stand on everything he believes in ever since.

He has been active and a trustee of another dozen organizations, but in addition to the University his great love is for his church and the YMCA. He has headed every YMCA campaign in his local community since 1954.

Red Blount looks like he's a man of sixty but I know for a fact that he must be closer to seventy-five. I asked him at what age a trustee should leave a board or whether there should be a mandatory retirement age. I know full well the danger of someone staying on too long and dominating board meetings with past victories and remembrances. There's the recital of all the things that had ever been tried before, and all the things that won't work. On the other hand, I have also watched a lot of trustees in action, half Red's age, who were already in the final stages of hardening of the creative arteries.

I am convinced that chronological age provides no indication of a person's value to the institution. It depends on the person.

"It's a sensitive question you ask," Red told me, "and I'm not certain I am totally without bias on the issue. I have had a couple of organizations extend their retirement age for me. They knew I would continue giving them money, at the same level, whether I was on the board or not —and so I don't believe that was a factor. They know I come regularly to meetings and that when I say I am going to do something, I do it. They know they can count on me and that I work very hard. As a trustee, I always have. I believe age is not a factor."

I asked him about his giving. In just about every campaign he's involved in, Red is the first and the largest donor.

"It's a strange thing. Whenever I give, it seems to come back to me. I really believe this is true.

"And it's interesting that you should ask me about this because just last week, my son and I were talking about the very same thing. We were talking about his recent gifts to his church and he told me how they somehow seemed to come back to him many times over. It's not magic. I believe there are ample biblical references that substantiate this.

"And there's another thing. The harder I seem to work on a project for one of my organizations, the better I seem to do personally. There is absolutely no rational explanation for this. All I can tell you is that it happens."

Jerome Stone is one who agrees with Blount—on all counts.

"If you have some money, share it. And if you have some time, give it. Do something worthwhile. You'll get it back many times over."

Stone is the founder and chairman of the Alzheimer's Association. The group provides the funds for research and education for this debilitating neurological disease.

When he founded the Association, Stone was chief executive officer of Stone Container Corporation, one of the largest in the country. He was younger, too. Today, he is seventy-six and just as vigorous as ever, and still giving an immense amount of time to the Alzheimer's Association. Since its fledging start, the Association now has 110 on its staff and 200 chapters.

Age is not a factor in judging a trustee's ability to serve. Being young in heart and spirit—that's what counts. And that has nothing to do with age.

21

TAKE YOUR BUSINESS HEAD ALONG

TOO OFTEN, BOARD MEMBERS ARE NOT courageous, entrepreneurial, or daring.

Even the most astute corporate executives, when they walk into a board room, often stop making wise business decisions. That's not my statement, although I find it commonly true. The comments come from a study we conducted among a large group of social agency executives.

That may sound severe. But wait!

In a similar study we conducted among 2000 corporate executives who serve on hospital boards, we asked these successful business leaders if they felt they exercised the same kind of astute, good business judgment in the hospital board room as they do with their own staff and in their own corporate offices. The response was fascinating. They think and react differently in the board meeting of their hospital.

One corporate executive told me: "I'm certain that

when I meet with the symphony board, I think and act differently. At the plant, I'm trained and expected to make fast, hard decisions. What I do affects the future of the company. At times I've got to be terribly tough. With my staff and around the office, I would be known as being pretty hard-nosed. But on the symphony board, I feel I have to be a little bit more restrained, a little bit more thoughtful, somewhat slower. After all, I'm dealing with a different kind of value system, a different culture, and different sorts of people."

Wait a moment! In today's topsy-turvy environment, with a rollercoaster economy, and a value system that is totally out of kilter—we need more hard-nosed, good business decisions than ever before.

In a trustee, you certainly want compassion, but mixed heartily with good judgment. Sensitivity and feeling combined heavily with business sense and a financial point of view. And lots of passion and commitment, of course. But practical and realistic goal-setting and objectives have to be met.

What you really want in a trustee is a combination of the compassion of a Mother Teresa with the business sense of a Lee Iacocca.

22

HOW TO KEEP OUT OF TROUBLE

A N OUTSIDER CAN SPOT it a mile away. I've seen it a hundred times. The organization is in serious trouble and the reason is obvious. The board is trying to do the staff's job. Or the Chair wants to play executive director.

Here's how it should work. The chief executive officer, through his or her staff, initiates programs, activities, and new designs and concepts. They do this with the assistance and wise judgment of board members and appropriate committee people.

Policy determination is the province of the board, and the board only.

Policy execution is the responsibility of the staff. And trustees are admonished not to meddle. There ought to be a "No Trespassing" sign firmly in place. And if you don't like the job the staff is doing in executing programs, activities, and policy—get a new staff. That's indeed the job of trustees.

It's a sure sign of problems when the Chair spends an inordinate amount of time talking with faculty members, physicians, or staff people. There's trouble brewing for sure.

In one of San Francisco's largest and most prestigious hospitals, for years the Chair of the board has had an office next to the office of the hospital administrator. The Chair spends hours each day in the office. That gives me the heeby-jeebies! It's really tough for a topflight administrator to exist in that kind of an environment. It can work—but it adds perplexity to an already difficult job.

In this kind of a situation, the chief executive officer must feel somewhat how a lamp post must feel about dogs!

Here's the key. Follow these principles and you'll never get into trouble.

Initiation: The staff, with great assistance from the board.

Determination: The board.

Execution: The staff—with careful evaluation and review from the board.
   And great applause from the board when a job is well done!

23

REWARDS

I F YOU WANT TO make the greatest investment possible of your time and skills, become a trustee. It will pay the most rewarding dividends you have ever had.

You join an extraordinary army of men and women who share with you in this business. And talk about "a growth industry" with unlimited potential. Why, there's absolutely no end to what you can do. Your product will reach hundreds, perhaps thousands and tens of thousands. It doesn't just happen—it is the result of creative thinking, strategic planning, and a very good marketing program. It takes all of that.

You're sending kids to camp, you're taking care of someone with cancer, you're thwarting delinquency, you're curing a patient, you're making it possible for someone to go to school. Whatever it is, your organization is doing it—and doing it with a style and effectiveness unlike that of any other organization.

Your investment is of monumental proportions. It's strange—you don't really spend a lot of time talking about "the bottom line." You understand that the rewards only come to you when your organization is effectively changing lives or saving lives.

24

ORIENTATION

Without exception, trustees should receive a thorough orientation before coming to their first meeting. This should include a complete tour of the facilities and departments. In addition, it should include presentations by some of the senior staff people, and an explanation of the procedural aspects of being a board member.

The orientation meeting provides the best opportunity possible to interpret what stewardship, trusteeship, and institutional responsibility are all about.

This kind of a session can be held at a retreat-type setting or at the organizations's headquarters. I prefer the latter because it provides easier access for a tour.

The orientation is most effectively done when new members have three hours or so alone, and then are joined for dinner or lunch by all trustees. It is an immensely satisfying and effective launching for a person's tenure in the organization. When the orientation doesn't happen, or is too casual, a valuable bonding opportunity is lost.

25

HOW TO BE
A STAR

A S A TRUSTEE, THERE are thirteen criteria you can use
to help measure your performance. You could add
other items, but they will not rate any higher than these.
The following are not listed in any order of priority.

1. You work at understanding your institution, its history, and its present program and outreach. You understand its mission and you measure everything the
institution does in relation to its philosophy of operation.

2. You are faithful about attending board and committee
meetings and you participate fully, openly, and with can-
dor.

3. You come carefully prepared for all board and committee meetings. This is especially true if you are asked to
make decisions that have a high impact on the future of the

organization and those it serves. You should not vote without proper understanding and preparation.

4. You are a roaring advocate! At every opportunity possible, you speak with enthusiasm and a certain ardor about the organization.

5. You bring to bear all of the influence possible to persuade others to act on behalf of the institution.

6. You settle for nothing less than the best. You make certain that all activities and offerings are of the highest quality possible. It is indeed a very strange phenomenon of trusteeship—when you refuse to accept anything but the very best, you most often get it.

7. You bring your business acumen into the board room. You make certain that your comments and your vote expresses good, sound judgment. You don't play "follow the leader" (unless, of course, you are the leader!). You decide what is the very best for the cause, and you fight for it. After the vote is taken, you act as an adult. If you simply can't tolerate the action that was taken and it becomes a matter you find near-impossible to deal with, you give serious consideration to leaving the board.

8. You develop a good understanding of the institutions that are in competition with yours, or are serving constituencies in the same way. You become acquainted with the marketing concept and you even become acquainted with such strange sounding word-combinations as Product, Price, and Place.

9. You volunteer! There are assignments that come up,

some that are difficult and fairly time-consuming—and you offer to take them on. At first, you may shock fellow trustees with your willingness. But after a short while, that kind of spirit catches on. It is contagious.

10. You give sacrificially. That means, you give to the very best of your ability. No one can or will ever tell you how much to give. But it is certainly expected that you do as much as you can because you are a trustee. And, you help get gifts from others—friends, business associates, and neighbors. At first, they may be tempted to duck you—but your enthusiasm will be so infectious they will find the cause irresistible.

11. You channel your ongoing skills into the work of the board. If you have an accounting background, you may wish to serve on the Finance Committee. Advertising folks would have a bent toward Public Relations.

12. You provide accord and acclaim for the good performance of staff. You have a right to expect the very best performance possible from your staff and chief executive officer The truth is, however, that not every organization has a staff that comes up to this high expectation. When yours does, let them know it. You'll be amazed at what wondrous things this can achieve.

13. To rate really high marks as a trustee, it may not be possible for you to serve on more than a few boards at one time. For some men and women, they cannot serve on more than one and still perform to the highest capacity. Ration your time and energy to those boards where you can give the most to the organizations you love the most. The pay-off will be tremendous.

26

REACHING *ARETE*

"**I**T'S THE RENT I pay."

A simple statement—and I've never heard it expressed so eloquently. I was talking with Thomas Conron, founder of the American Hardware Company in Danville, Illinois. He is a bright and vital seventy-four years old and continues to serve as an active trustee on four major boards in Danville. He has been providing this same kind of dedicated involvement in his beloved community for the past forty years.

"Why do you do it, Tom?" I asked. "Why do you keep serving? What has kept you so active? You have been heavily involved over the years in so many worthwhile projects. You could be taking life easy now."

"This community has been so wonderful to me, and my father before me, and my grandfather before him. I can't get over how blessed I am and how lucky I have been all my years. This town has been so good to me.

"I guess I keep on serving..." There was a pause. "I guess I keep on serving, because that's the rent I pay."

It's like climbing the highest peak. You have answered the summons, and you have not been found wanting.

It's not always easy. It takes abiding and unbounded enthusiasm. There must be a passion, dedication, and zeal for the task, the burden, the travail, and the responsibility.

Being a trustee should bring out the very best within you. It means reaching the highest level, a standard of excellence the Greeks called *Arete*. It means to function as you are supposed to, to serve others, to meet all of life's responsibilities, and to achieve your own very best.

The great joy of a trustee is to ignite the spark which glows, and ultimately lights the way for the organization. And as a trustee, you rekindle that spark when it begins to flicker.

There are some men and women who for one reason or another do not give of themselves. They don't serve on boards, they don't get involved, they live in their own world of selfish stagnation. You know some of these folks, and it's hard to understand why they haven't discovered the great joy of serving others. What soaring exhilaration they are missing. And then there are those, just like you, who strengthen and empower society, just by being the kind of people they are.

Tom, he's seventy-four years old and still serving. Those who study this sort of thing say there is medical evidence that it is what keeps him young. In the midst of his winter, he has learned that there is an invincible summer.

He pays his rent, just like you.

27

ORGANIZATIONAL MOMENTUM

I T IS DIFFICULT TO define, puzzling to identify, and impossible to measure. But it's there—a very real thing. In your institution, momentum is everything. It makes all things possible. It converts individual trustees into a team of dedicated devotion. It lifts and transforms men and women beyond a personal interest and unites them in a common cause.

The board is responsible for monitoring this elusive quality called momentum. If it is accelerating, you can sense it, you can feel it. If it is slipping, trustees need to roll up their sleeves and do something about it.

Momentum requires the intrepidity to say, "We must do better." It is an arduous pledge the board must make. But where there is no pain, there is no momentum. It requires energy-busting force and indomitable courage, an unrelenting quest to break the rigid bonds of institutional paralysis. It demands the highest of ideals.

An organization with momentum has an impelling and infectious surge. An undisciplined fervor for the fray and venture. Forward, always forward. Advancing. Achieving. Accelerating.

Momentum doesn't just happen. It requires the electrifying force of a leader and the ever present vigilance of the board. Trustees must be single-minded and unswerving in the pursuit of an objective, with an ardor and zeal which knows no bounds. Momentum demands a raging vision and passion to be the best.

In your organization, momentum ignites the atmosphere and sends an electrical charge through all you do. It invigorates the spirit of trustees who are charged with the institution's destiny.

But momentum is fragile and easily lost. And once lost, difficult to regain. In some situations, impossible. That is why trustees must monitor and guide as best they can the momentum of their organization. Because in your institution, momentum is everything. It drives, directs, and determines your organization's destiny.

28

HOW YOU TELL WHAT'S IMPORTANT

NO MATTER WHAT ANYONE says to the contrary, one way to consider your organization's priorities is to look over the committee rosters. See which committees have the most influential among your board and those who would be considered of the highest leadership capacity. If most serve on the Finance Committee or the Investment committee—you have a pretty good idea of where the organization places its priority. If, on the other hand, they serve on the Patient Care Committee, the Academic Committee, or the Program Services Committee—this speaks eloquently about your focus and thrust.

All of the work of the board is important. An effective committee structure makes the organization resonate with vitality. But a board that puts all of its leadership, power, influence, and affluence into, let's say, the Finance Committee, may end up at the end of the year with a balanced budget—but a severe program deficit.

The engine that drives your institutional train is the program, the service. The funds fuel the engine. The train, the engine, the fuel—they are all essential in keeping the organization on track.

29

GO AHEAD AND SQUEEZE

ONE OF THE GREATEST trustees I've worked with was Fred Braemer. For years, he was Chairman of the board of Albert Einstein Medical Center in Philadelphia. He had a favorite expression he used when there was a tough decision to be made, one that would require a great deal of determination. He would ask: "Is the juice worth the squeeze?" If it was, his resolve and devotion to the effort was boundless.

Board members should bring to their trusteeship and to each board meeting a probing, challenging, question-demanding mind.

What is our organization achieving? Are we meeting our mission? What are our dreams?

This requires resolute soul-searching. Montaigne said: "Virtue will have nothing to do with ease. It seeks a rough and thorny path." There will be times when your trusteeship will seem rougher and thornier than you really care to tackle!

Being an effective trustee takes determination—abiding and unbounded determination. What is required is the dedication to purpose, the spirit of enterprise, and the tenacity of high resolve.

It takes, also, an unswerving commitment to the cause.

The world cries out for help in meeting needs that are vexing and complex. There are more questions than there are answers. The world needs hands and hearts to reach out. For the thousands who cry out but are not heard, it is one minute until midnight. In times like these, for a board to spend undue time reviewing the minutes of the last meeting instead of discussing how to save lives—there's trouble.

"Decisions can be difficult," says John Gardner. "At times, agonizing."

Group wisdom doesn't come easily. Sound strategy, proper funding, and difficult decisions can become hard-fought battles. It takes boundless faith. And determination and a toughness of mind. At times, the trustee path seems paved with boulders instead of pebbles.

It helps to have a child's attitude. A youngster doesn't get discouraged because a bubble bursts. They frantically begin working to blow another one.

Being a trustee is a marathon, long and at times exhausting. Often, at close view, the finish line never seems to be in sight. Unrewarding and unfulfilling. But then, at last, you break the tape, you cross the finish line. You have achieved your destination. You have reached your objective. You have won. You have won. That's exhilarating!

Why is it, with all that is required, why is it that busy men and women are willing to become trustees? Because—the juice is worth the squeeze.

30

BE WILLING
TO DARE

F OR AN INSTITUTION TO grow and flourish it must be inherently vital, incessantly curious, aggressively courageous. Hungry for innovation, quick to respond to human need, willing to fight for a social agenda. Eager to face head-on challenges of the times.

This happens only with trustees willing to dare and challenge the status quo.

Trustees must be able to stand back, take a piercing hard look, and be willing to make some difficult decisions if necessary. Not a job for the faint-hearted! But anything less serves the organization poorly. History will not deal kindly with trustees who are willing to accept things as they are, instead of examining how things should be.

Trustees can assure the progress and vitality of the organization with ideas ahead of their time. Visions of exhilaration and faith. Discarding the old for the uncharted new. The development, encouragement, and the support of new ideas are important to your organization because they direct and determine your destiny. In an era when the only thing that is constant is change, new ideas are your lifeline.

In "The Devil's Disciple," George Bernard Shaw says it best of all. Note this well, board members: ". . . Some men see things as they are and say why. I dream things that never were and say why not." Let that be your hymn: "Why not?"

31

HOLDING WATER

I T IS QUITE CLEAR. The chief executive officer reports to the board of trustees. The evaluation of the chief's work is one of the primary and overriding responsibilities of the board. Except in the most unusual of situations, all of the other staff, professional and otherwise, report finally to the chief.

Trustees, however, should demonstrate in all they do and in all their decisions, a certain passion, concern, and understanding for the entire staff of the organization—no matter how large it is.

John W. Gardner has written of this in words so eloquent, they cannot be improved. The paragraph deserves printing and framing for every manager's office.

"There may be excellence or shoddiness in every line of human endeavor. We must learn to honor excellence (indeed, to demand it) in every socially accepted human activity, however humble the activity, and to scorn shoddiness, however exalted the activity. An excellent plumber is infinitely more admirable than an incompetent philosopher. The society which scorns excellence in plumbing because plumbing is a humble activity and tolerates shoddiness in philosophy because it is an exalted activity will have neither good plumbing nor good philosophy. Neither its pipes nor its theories will hold water."

32

YOU CAN TELL IF YOU PASS

I HAVE DESIGNED A "test" that helps determine how competent a trustee you are. I call it: PASS.

Policymaker, Advocate, Skilled, and Sustainer. The effective board member combines all four.

A trustee, foremost, has the responsibility for governance. That overrides any other single duty. No one else can determine policy. It cannot be transferred, delegated, or abdicated.

The trustee is an Advocate. You carry the flag! More than anyone, you are the goodwill ambassador for the organization and tell its story whenever and wherever possible.

At the University of Tennessee, Cornelia Hodges told me: "Honestly, I would get embarrassed. John and I would go for drinks or to a dinner, and the next thing I knew, he had someone cornered and was telling them about his beloved library. I was afraid that we'd never get invited anywhere anymore. But somehow, people always understood.

He was passionate about the place and he managed to get everyone just as excited. And the invitations for dinner kept coming."

You have a major role to champion the cause, and as a trustee, you do it with unending gusto. Your advocacy is something you do with unbounded and uninhibited enthusiasm—you are the institution's chief friend-raiser.

Trustees bring skills to the organization and to meetings. Professionally and in their "real life," they may be educators, attorneys, accountants, or whatever. These can become skills that are used to great effect by the organization. But don't be afraid to speak up—if you are an accountant or a banker, the last committee you want to serve on may be the finance committee. If you're an attorney, it isn't necessarily right for the organization to expect you to do all of its legal work free. On the other hand, it can be a serious conflict of interest if you are an insurance agent and you benefit from the sale of policies.

And as a trustee, you have the responsibility to sustain its program. You give and you influence others to give. I believe that trusteeship assumes a concern and a commitment for funding. It may not be the institution you give your greatest support to, but it should surely be among the top of those you love and care about. Once again, the venerable trustee admonition: "If you as a board member don't care, why should anyone else." It is surely one of the great verities of trusteeship. As a director, you should give as much as you possibly can—of course, proportional to your means and ability. But whatever you can do, you should. This may pose a problem to some who serve on three or four boards, or half a dozen. Indeed it does. And it need only impose the question as to whether you are able to serve and support all.

But PASS wasn't too rigorous a test. You already meet the four criteria. And you're having a great time and you're making the organization glow and glitter with activity. You pass!

33

THREE TIMES,
AND THEY'RE OUT

I T HAS BEEN MY experience that if a new trustee misses their first three meetings, they will never become involved. They will be lost forever. I have known of no exceptions to this.

This makes it incumbent on the Chair and the chief officer to see to it that a new trustee is called on immediately following the first meeting they miss. Find a way to bring them to the second meeting or have a friend pick them up.

I assure you, if they miss the second meeting, you're in serious trouble. Make certain the Chair intercedes before you get past the point of no return.

34

EXCELLENCE IS NO ACCIDENT

A HIGH LEVEL OF excellence is within the reach of every organization. But it doesn't just happen.

Excellence is achieved in an institution only as a result of the trustees' unrelenting and vigorous insistence on the highest standards of performance. It requires an unswerving expectancy of quality from all the staff and volunteers.

Best of all, it is contagious. It infects and affects everyone in the organization. When you design a road map for high quality, you chart the direction for everything you do.

Once achieved, excellence has a talent for permeating every aspect of the life of the organization.

But you must pay the price. Excellence demands commitment and tenacious dedication from trustees and all the leaders of the organization. It is what is accepted and expected. It must be nourished and continually reviewed and renewed. It is a never-ending process of striving and searching. The trustees' search for excellence requires a spirit of mission and boundless energy.

Excellence inspires. It electrifies. It extends to every phase of the organization's life. It unleashes an impact which influences every program, every activity, every committee, every staff person.

To instill a high level of excellence in your institution is difficult. To sustain it, even more so. Trustees need imagination and vigor. But most of all, trustees need adaptability and discipline.

Excellence is your organization's life-line. It is the only answer to apathy and inertia. Once it becomes the expected standard of performance, it develops a life of its own, a fiercely driving and motivating philosophy of operation. It guides everything you do. Excellence is a state of mind put into action. When a climate of excellence exists in your organization, all things are success-driven. Your staff work, volunteer leadership, finances, and program— they all feel the impact and the stimulation and the inspiration.

As a trustee, you understand that excellence in your organization is important—because it is everything.

35

YOU GET OUT
WHEN YOU PUT IN

I SPOKE TO SIDNEY Val Smith recently, and asked why he has served on the vestry of his church for so long a period.

Mr. Smith, until recently, owned the largest real estate management firm in Houston. He served as Senior Warden of the affluent and important St. John's Episcopal parish for three decades. I heard one Houstonian refer to St. John's as the parish "of which there is no whicher"! That's a very special category.

"Why have you given so much time to the church? Why do you give it so much energy and service?"

Smith's response was: "Because the church is serving me so much more than I am serving it. In life you get so much more out of something when you put something back into it."

Smith also serves as Chair of the Cullen Foundation Education Trust. As a grantor, he always looks and evaluates what an institution's board is giving before the Foundation decides to make its grant. "If the organization's directors aren't interested enough to give, why should the Foundation? I'm on the board of the Episcopal High School and we are going into our third campaign—this time for around $15 million. We have a number of priests who serve on that board. They may not have as much to give as some of the other trustees. But I've told our board people that we all need to give. In this case, and even with the priests, it may not matter how much—but it is important that everybody gives so we let the world know that we are all heavily involved."

Earl L. Gadbery agrees with Smith about the importance of trustee giving. For nineteen years, he led the largest corporation foundation in the world. ALCOA has assets of over $250 million. For all those years, Earl has been a voice of corporate consciousness, a towering advocate of philanthropy, and one of the nation's most highly regarded spokesman for corporate citizenship.

He told me that when he considered requests from an institution for a grant from ALCOA, one of the things he always did was to review the list of trustees to see who might have a direct corporate connection. If they did, he would always ask what that person's corporation had done for the campaign program. His feeling was that if the trustee's own corporation did not support the program, why should ALCOA. He expected trustees to be heavily involved.

Heavily and heavenly involved!

God loves a cheerful giver. We know that to be true. It is written in the Book. Nowhere does it say that heaven frowns on a trustee who doesn't give. But I strongly suspect that God doesn't take any particular pleasure in those folks either.

36

SOME OVERRIDING PRINCIPLES

NONE OF THESE WILL surprise you. But note the principles well. They are irrefutable.

1. You will find it easier to recruit and keep good board members if you have a successful operation. No one wants to serve as a trustee to help save the sinking Titanic.

2. Strong board members are attracted to strong staff. The chief executive officer helps define and determine the type of person who chooses to serve on the board. The more effective the chief, the more effective the board. The force of the leader determines the stratum of the trustees.

3. Fundraising cannot be conducted successfully without trustees who are influential, affluential, and affirmative. If fundraising is significant to your institution—and it is to most—you need board members who can give or influence large gifts, and are unabashed advocates for your work.

4. Excellence doesn't just happen. It requires a shared

commitment on the part of both staff and board to be nothing less than the best.

5. A board that is unwilling to pay effective staff appropriate salaries often gets the kind of staff it deserves.

6. Trustees who do not prepare properly for board meetings should never complain about the institution's focus or direction.

7. A whole world of capable men and women is waiting to be asked to serve on your board. They are magnificent people and will contribute mightily in every way to the work of the organization. They are just waiting to be asked. You will be hurt more by those who were not asked and would have said *yes*—than by those who say *no*. Follow this rule and you will have an outstanding board.

8. Combine a Methodist's sense of righteousness with the zeal of a Joan of Arc.

37

FIND YOUR *KAIROS*

T HE GREEKS HAVE TWO terms they use for the word "time".

One is the word *chronos*. That's the root of our word for chronology—the measure of time, hours, minutes, and seconds.

The other Greek word for time is *kairos*. That has quite a different meaning, not easily described. It is best understood as that very precious moment in time when a person or a group has the opportunity to undertake and achieve great things. It is a moment of magic, not often presented in a lifetime, when towering victories can be achieved.

Every organization has its own *kairos*.

But these great moments do not often come announced. This means that you must be an opportunity seeker. You must expect opportunities and prospect for them. And note that the evidence is quite clear on this point—those who seek and expect opportunities, get them.

Right now, this can be your *kairos*. This is your organization's day of unconquerable opportunities. Never were expectations higher. Never the need greater. There has never been a time when you have been in such perfect position to achieve such extraordinary results.

Embrace the opportunity. Today is the day. *Carpe Diem.* Seize the day!

38

NEW IDEAS ARE THE LIFELINE

E INSTEIN SAID: "IT TAKES action. I never have faith in an idea that I came upon while sitting down." Perhaps that's why there's such a paucity of ideas at board meetings.

Ideas have lit every lamp, built every church, started every hospital, made every discovery, and ignited every single act of progress. It is the spark that blazes every new trail of growth. In your organization, ideas are the priceless ingredient. It is what transforms a good organization into a premier one.

But it's no easy task, the business of transferring an idea from one mind to another, from one committee to the board. It can be the most hazardous of human endeavors, because you cannot pre-suppose the existence of a receptive mind.

Growth can be achieved in your organization only through constant challenge and change, discarding tired and worn-out activities that have outlived their usefulness, instilling new ideas of dazzling force.

This is why I resist strongly the policy of a required age limit for board membership. I have seen many trustees in their 70s and yes, beyond, who demonstrate untempered enthusiasm. They seem to understand that every great advance is the result of an audacious idea. And I have seen, too, young trustees in their 30s and 40s—with locked minds, who gag and gasp at the thought of anything that is new. The truth is that a trifling, trepid mind of any age cannot accept anything new, nor accomplish anything great or good.

It is your responsibility as a trustee to be receptive. That's the key—to be willing to listen and study. Analyze and assess. And then take action. You'll know when it's a good idea. Like Emily Dickinson, you'll be able to say: "I know it's great if I feel that the top of my head has just taken off."

As a trustee, you accept that fact that no existing truth is sacred, no roots so deeply planted that they cannot be pulled up. Hardly a principle calculated to give comfort to the fearful. It requires self-inspection and self-criticism. That's difficult. And it also requires, foresight, faith, and flaming courage.

Trustees must resist the clinking clutter of dead customs and traditions, disdain the barnacles of obsolete service, and reject outmoded programs. An institution can make unlimited progress if it has determined trustees, creative men and women who are ahead of their times in their ideas.

It requires trustees and staff locked in a creative environment of deliberate receptivity and wild abandonment. Trustees and staff working together, seeking new limits of the possible, and then going beyond.

A new outreach, a new direction, new ideas—they can be intricately delicate. Fragile. Easily shattered, torn apart, still-born by the attack of a trifling mind. Destroyed by the trustee-quibbler who is a spectator at the sidelines. The first trustee who says: "We can't do it here"—should be dealt with accordingly. Although I warn you that flogging is no longer in style!

The board that gives advocacy to new ideas unlocks tomorrow, breaks through old barriers, and bursts beyond the imponderable to new horizons.

As a trustee, you understand that the future begins today with the genesis and genius of ideas. This creation requires the faith to persevere and the spirit to overcome any adversity. Faith and spirit—you will need them to respond to objections and meet challenges head-on.

Go ahead. Dare to discard the old for the uncharted new. The development, encouragement, and support of new ideas are important to your institution because they direct and determine your destiny.

In today's world, when the only thing that is constant is change, new ideas are your organization's lifeline. Be one with Euripides: "Take the path that no man before has walked."

39

FINDING THE RIGHT TIME

YOUR INSTITUTION COULD use more money. Without even knowing you or your organization, I feel I'm fairly safe in that statement. No crystal ball needed!

And I can assure you, also, that there is no "perfect time to raise money." You will find that there is no such thing as a time when all possible factors are in your favor.

This may be somewhat of a surprise, but economic conditions are not a prime factor in your organization's ability to raise funds—for either annual operations or major capital campaigns. As a matter of fact, philanthropy has been one of the most stable factors in our economy, year-in and year-out.

The plain fact is that in good times and in bad, Americans continue to give to causes of merit and compelling worthiness.

The pursuit of goodness and caring concern of the American people—there is nothing like it in all of history.

And the same loving care and concern is there for your organization, just waiting to be called on.

It may seen like a contradiction but the evidence is clear —when times are difficult and traumatic, Americans respond with even greater dedication, generosity, and a genuine sense of sacrifice. And it's there, waiting for your organization. There is a whole host of friends who love you. They may not know they are friends, and they may not yet know they love you. But I promise you, they are out there, just waiting to hear your story.

It's a wondrous thing about Americans. They support those organizations they believe in. They have never failed. They allow nothing to interfere with their fervor. And when they hear of your great work, they will support your worthwhile cause.

But you must prepare, you must lay the proper foundation, you must develop a plan so daringly creative and dramatic that it penetrates the heart and unshackles the passion.

Whether for sustained funds or major capital gifts, you will be successful—but only when you are ready. That means total commitment on the part of every board member. Every board member! And it means developing a plan which enables you to reach out to those who already know of your good work and those who should.

Now this all seems like quite an oversimplification, but that's really how easy it is. But it does require a scourging commitment on the part of trustees. And it requires a plan that is conceived with brilliant innovation and implemented with dogged precision.

A commitment and a plan. It is a fail-proof combination.

40

BLESSED IS
THE CHAIR

A COLLEGE PRESIDENT TOLD ME THE other day that the board chairperson who can smile when things go wrong...has thought of a dean to blame it on!

There is an organization called the Volunteer Consulting Group. It provides consulting services for trustee recruitment and management. The executive director is Brooke W. Mahoney.

In a recent article, Ms. Mahoney asked: "Who in their right mind would be Chair of a nonprofit hospital or museum board right now?" That is an astounding comment coming from one who should be celebrating trusteeship.

I say who in their right mind?—hundreds of thousands of men and women right now, that's who! Men and women who are concerned about their community. Men and women who are willing to make the commitment of time and energy because they care greatly about the institution.

Who in their right mind indeed!

I'll tell you who. Men and women who understand there is no other nation in the world with the array of activities and services provided by the nonprofits. Men and women who are concerned about saving lives and changing lives. Men and women who understand that the nonprofit is in reality the fabric and character of this nation. The men and women who recognize that it is their institution that gives nourishment and sustenance to those in need.

I say—blessed are the Chairpersons, and in heaven they shall stand on the right hand of the martyrs.

41

WHAT YOU CAN'T DUCK

NO MATTER HOW IT is delegated, you and other trustees have the final responsibility for the proper funding of your institution. For many organizations, that means that board members must play the major role in fundraising.

Wait a minute. Don't skip to the next section!

I know you may not want to be reminded about your responsibility for fundraising, but you'd better read on!

You can go out and hire "a fundraiser"—but that probably won't get the job done. I know you're not pleased to hear that. No matter how good the development person, and there are thousands of really good ones in the field—they are going to need your help.

In most cases, it pays to have a full-time person who carries the portfolio for fundraising. If you don't have such a person, it will really be helpful to make a careful assessment to see if the idea makes sense for your organization. In most cases, it does.

If you don't have someone on your staff who is given the assignment for fundraising, chances are it will end up being done by your executive director. Or more likely—not being done by your executive director. The problem is that the executive's agenda is already so full, fundraising won't get much attention, no matter how important it is.

By the way, if you do have a person who is supposed to do the fundraising, and they split time between that and another responsibility—say, public relations—I can assure you that the fundraising won't get much attention. In every case I know and in every study I have done, I find that when a staff person divides their workload, fundraising suffers the most. The idea sounds good and it even looks impressive on those organizational charts we consultants love doing—but it simply doesn't work. No exceptions.

Hire a full-time person. In the end, it should not cost you. It should pay. And the dividends and long-range benefits will be immense.

But no matter how you are staffed, the ultimate responsibility for fundraising is yours, the trustee.

You may decide to have a development committee. And that makes sense. The group should meet regularly and be headed by one of the strongest board members you have. But no matter how active and effective this committee, the final responsibility for fundraising is the entire board's.

A lot of organizations form a foundation. In some situations, this is an effective and valid concept. Some of these foundations function very much as a committee of the board, while others are free-standing, at arms-length. There are valid reasons for both, and you should evaluate which is more effective for your organization. The important thing is to have more people helping you with this essential endeavor and some of your most effective leaders providing focused time and energy. But no matter how you end up doing it, nothing changes. The board has the final responsibility for the success of fundraising.

You may be a trustee of an organization with a large development office. I know of some with several hundred on the fundraising staff. Whatever the size of the development staff—the final responsibility for fundraising and having adequate institutional funds rests with the trustees.

As a trustee, there are a host of functions and activities you need not concern yourself with. Don't get bogged down in those kinds of things. But as far as fundraising is concerned, that's an institutional imperative that you cannot delegate. It won't go away and it needs your utmost attention and concern.

I haven't discovered many men or women who join a board because they love fundraising, and just can't wait to get started. And I have uncovered very few, also, who queue up for fundraising assignments.

What I have found is that once a trustee does get involved, they find it to be a rather enjoyable experience. Downright fulfilling and rewarding. They find that it can be one of the most exhilarating experiences they undertake as a trustee. In fact, I have had some say that it's a real high point—knowing that through their direct efforts, funds have become available to perform some of the very significant ministries of their organization.

Colette Murray is the dynamic Vice President for Philanthropy at the Henry Ford Health System in Detroit— the largest single system in the country. Colette told me the story of how Martha Firestone Ford joined the board of the health system. Then she was asked to serve on the Committee On Philanthropy. Mrs. Ford told Colette: "I don't mind being a member of the committee, but I certainly won't call on anyone for a gift. Please don't ask me to do that. I hate that sort of thing."

But Mrs. Ford became extremely interested in the work of the alcohol treatment program of the hospital. She became involved as a volunteer and provided major leadership. Colette then asked Mrs. Ford to join her on a call for a donation. Martha Ford started, on a tentative and tenuous basis. She really didn't like asking friends for gifts.

But she was so involved in the alcohol treatment program and so dedicated to its cause, she continued making calls. Colette says: "Now Mrs. Ford is unstoppable. She loves it. She does it because she is successful and because she feels so strongly about the importance of the program and how effectively the donations are being used."

Go ahead. Try it. Work at it. Ask another trustee or a staff member to join you in making a call. The gift you get can make a consequential difference in your organization. It can help save a life. There's no greater high.

THIRTEEN WAYS
TO HELP
FUNDRAISE

1. YOU RECOMMEND influential and affluential men and
women to serve with you on the board. The more
powerful the board, the more you will raise. Introducing
these new people has a long-term effect of salubrious proportions.

2. Make certain the organization exercises good stewardship, prudence with its funds, and fiscal stability. No one
wants to support an institution that is in a constant state of
financial implosion.

3. Be alert to the momentum and the success of the organization. Everyone likes to back a winner. The bandwagon
principle will work to your great advantage.

4. Get heavily involved in all concerns that are ancillary
to fundraising. During the course of the year, you will have

ample opportunity to review promotional material, mail appeals, newsletters, drafts of case statements, and so forth. Spend whatever time is necessary to make certain that what the institution does or sends out represents you and the organization in a way that makes you proud.

5. Be insistent that the organization is doing an effective job of telling its story to all of its constituencies, particularly those who are or should be donors. See that there is a program for interpretation and cultivation. Don't leave it to chance or think that someone else is doing it. Ask questions. Make certain that there is a structured strategy and that it is being implemented.

6. Introduce influentials to the organization. Arrange for key people to come to the organization for a visit. Have them meet with staff or other board members to talk about the great work of your organization. This can be done by inviting just one of your friends. But it is just as effective to arrange for small group meetings of four or five. Get the staff to help you with the arrangements and the scheduling. These small "roundtables" are one of the most effective ways of quietly selling the organization.

7. Be a roaring enthusiast. Tell everyone. Tell your friends and neighbors about the exciting work your organization is doing. Tell your business associates, your hairdresser, the butcher, the bridge club, the person you play golf with, and the candlestick maker. The ripple effect will pay off. I believe unreservedly in the seven-network theory. Tell seven sources how strongly you feel about the organization and it will result in a gift. I promise it works.

8. Help with special events, auctions, and all sorts of

fundraising programs. Yes, even raffles! I'm not a great believer in these programs. My strong feeling is that all of the time and energy that goes into these affairs could be better and more productively placed asking someone for gifts. But in the end, these can be public relations benefits and produce important dollars. Perhaps most importantly, if handled properly, it can generate a lot of new friends for the organization.

Don't be a spectator. Get fully involved. I had a board member say to me the other day: "I told my wife that instead of spending all of that time trying to sell tickets for a table at the auction, and wasting all of that time trying to get some items to auction off, we ought to just make a donation to the hospital." I told him that he probably ought to do both.

9. Every chance you have, pass on names of men and women. I had one board member tell me: "I never miss an opportunity. I carry around 3 by 5 cards for just that purpose. During the course of the day, every time I think of someone who should be added to our mailing list, I jot down the name. If I know the address, fine. But if I don't, I let the staff worry about it. You'd be surprised in the course of a week how many names I come up with." It's just a matter of deciding you are going to do it, thinking about doing it, and doing it! I imagine that every successful salesperson comes up with their own prospect list in pretty much the same way.

10. Help in reviewing names of giving sources. In some cases, you may not be the right person to make a contact for a gift, but you know or can recommend someone who is. Or you help in developing a strategy for making a call. Perhaps also deciding how much the organization should ask for.

11. Board members should review the names of those who have made gifts, and decide what is the most appropriate way of acknowledging the donation and demonstrating appreciation. You can't thank a donor too much or too often.

Note this as one of the truisms in friendraising and fundraising: You can't thank enough!

One of the effective ways acknowledgment and recognition are handled by boards is to list all of the donations that have come in since the last board meeting and review the names. This is best done on a flat-list. If you're sensitive about showing the amounts, don't. But take whatever time is necessary to look over the names and decide who will make the contact. Don't worry if you have more than one board member who calls or sends a letter. You can't thank too much, not if it is done effectively.

If you're on the board of an organization such as The Lutheran Laymen's League, or World Vision, or the National Easter Seal Society—the organization is receiving several thousand gifts each week. You couldn't possibly review that long a listing. But you could indeed pick out those donors where the gift was of a substantial size. Pick a level and use that as the floor.

12. Make your own gift. This is essential, so note it well. Every board member must be a donor. If you don't give, why should anyone else? Only you can determine the amount. But the determination to give should not be an option.

13. Ask others to give. You just knew I would finally get to this. As a trustee, and as an advocate, the role you play in asking others to share in the venture is of the highest order. You may need help—use the staff and other trustees.

I've heard trustees say they have tried calling on someone for a lift and they just don't like it. Some have even been stronger. "I hate it! I hate it!"

Something's wrong. Asking others to share in a great venture should be enjoyable. Asking others to help support a program that changes lives or save lives—that should be rewarding. It really can be exciting. Get a few board members and the staff to talk with you about some prospects and decide on a strategy and who should make the call.

But I warn you! Once you get started and you feel the exhilaration of getting the gift, you will never be able to stop. You will lust for it!

43

WHERE GIFTS GO

J UST RECENTLY, WALTER H. Annenberg presented $1 billion worth of paintings to the Metropolitan Museum of Art in New York. No modest gift, that!

Annenberg is former Ambassador to the Court of King James and very likely the most significant philanthropist in the history of this nation. Several years ago, his gift of $200 million to the University of Pennsylvania represented the largest donation ever made to an institution by a living individual.

Why did he make this most recent gift to the Metropolitan?

A number of other museums across the country were in hot pursuit of those fifty-three paintings. And several were certain they had an excellent chance. The National Gallery of Art in Washington is celebrating its 50th Anniversary and felt that because of its national orientation and focus, and the mid-century commemoration, it would get the nod.

Philadelphia is Annenberg's home city, where he was raised and grew up. It has an excellent museum and its staff felt very positive about the acquisition.

Annenberg now lives in Rancho Mirage, outside of Los Angeles. Over the years, Annenberg has befriended the Los Angeles County Museum of Art. The group there felt certain they would be the choice.

But in the end, Ambassador Annenberg gave his collection to the New York Metropolitan Museum of Art. His rationale is worthy of note. He said the gift was made because of "the character of the institution and the people running it."

He says many factors were involved in the decision, but the most important was that he was particularly influenced by the method and procedure the Metropolitan uses in selecting its trustees, and the time and the commitment board members give to the work of the Museum. Annenberg says that the trustees give sacrificially of both their time and their funds—and he was really impressed with that kind of dedication.

Does the same attitude and dedication prevail among trustees for institutions of perhaps less distinction than the Metropolitan? Or with gifts of lesser amounts?

The answer is a resounding *yes*.

I was involved recently in interviewing fifty men and women who had each made a gift of $1 million or more to institutions of their choice. Most of the group had made many more than one gift of this size. These were depth interviews, all lasting at least a day and some longer than that. What I found was emphatic, but not totally surprising.

The men and women in my study group gave because

they believed in the mission of the institution. There was no other factor that was nearly as consequential. Of course! No one gives if they do not believe in the work and the thrust of the organization.

Close behind that factor was a regard and an esteem for the board and staff. Of course! No one will give a major gift, a gift of any size, if they do not have complete confidence and faith in the team that guides the destiny of the institution.

It is an awesome responsibility you assume in your trusteeship. And a burden of some financial weight.

The institution that receives support and garners the gifts and grants, and is able to attract influential leadership —those organizations have trustees who merit confidence and support.

Ah, those magnificent works of art. Cézanne, Degas, Gauduin, Manet, Matisse, Monet, Picasso, Renoir, Toulouse-Lautrec, and van Gogh. In the future, you will see them at the Metropolitan. Thanks to the dedication and devotion of the Museum's trustees.

And your organization will receive the funds it needs because of your commitment. It may not measure up to a Renoir or a van Gogh, but being a really effective trustee is a fine art indeed.

WHERE QUALITY
RESIDES

A H, THE TEMPTATION IS great—but keep your hands out of the operation! Trustees are not to manage the institution, but to make certain that it is managed well.

Among the most consequential factors that make your institution great is the search and striving for excellence. And this must be a shared passion—trustees and the staff working together, locked in an unreasonably obsessive and driving desire for the highest quality possible, joined at the hips and pocketbooks.

Stephen E. Weil is Deputy Director of the Hirshorn Museum & Sculpture Garden in Washington. He is considered an authority on trusteeship. He says: "Trustees don't understand that an executive director can keep an institution on budget, raise substantial funds, and still run a perfectly lousy organization. What's missing from the equation is an indication of the institution's quality."

This passion for excellence must be shared, a total dedication of both staff and board. It cannot exist, one without the other. It is an imperative of the organization not easily adopted, and not achieved without rigid resolve. The drive for excellence is the glue that binds staff and trustees. It requires intrepid and continual self-examination.

Your organization reaches the highest pinnacle of fulfillment when it is consumed in the pursuit of excellence. It is a course not to be determined casually. For once the decision is made, it establishes a pattern and a pace that is unrelenting and unending.

Trustees and staff should follow Louis Armstrong's admonition: "Don't do nothing halfway, else you find yourself dropping more than can be picked up."

45

LIVE LONGER

Trustees live longer. And not only that, they're happier and more fulfilled.

Now I admit, that must appear to be a bodacious leap of modest and untested medical documentation to a totally unreasonable and biased conclusion. But consultants are allowed to do that!

Follow my logic. It is a well known fact, medically substantiated, that men and women who enjoy life, and are having fun, and feel fulfilled—these folks live longer. Typically, they abound with energy and zeal. They reach out to those around them. Their joy of life is infectious.

That's pretty well documented. Read on.

I am convinced that hard work does not kill. Quite the contrary. I am certain, also, that stress does not cause death. The right amount of stress has a salubrious effect. We all need stress.

What causes death is inactivity and a void of meaning in

life. That's death. For this type of sideline spectator, atrophy produces a lingering existence which is worse than sudden death. You've heard the axiom: "I would rather burn out than rust out." Well, the "rust out" type of person is typically not the kind who serves on a board.

With men and women who do not care deeply about something, there takes place a hardening of the spiritual arteries. They get caught in a pattern of living where their existence becomes plain vanilla. Take the advice of Auntie Mame. She said that life is a wonderful banquet, but the trouble is that most folks never take part in the feast.

For those who are willing to give their time for the good of others and for a great cause, there somehow appears an astonishing source of energy, an extraordinary sense of revitalization and renewal. Suddenly, there is no limit. This energy, this zest comes because they love what they are doing.

This should be no surprise to trustees who serve their beloved organizations. Without agony or apology, they give selflessly of their time and funds. They find reward and fulfillment that money cannot buy. They find meaning and significance in what they do. They know they make a contribution which is uniquely their own.

We are all captured within a certain prison of our own making. You have all heard the locked-in excuses. *There isn't time. I have too much to do already. When I serve, it costs me money. I don't like asking others to give or to help.* To break out of the prison, that's where the real life is.

To stand for something, to have compassion and passion for something larger than yourself. That's the life. To care greatly and deeply about others. Ah, that's what it is all about.

And because those who serve most, enjoy life most—I am convinced they live longer. All right, all you Doubting

Thomases. Challenge me if you choose. But those who serve most, they are certainly the happiest. Of that there can be no doubt.

You've heard that there's no one who lives longer than a widow who has remembered your organization in her will. There's a corollary to that: There's no one who lives longer or enjoys life more—than one who gives their life to help others.

And so, dear trustee: take on the assignment, chair the committee, work on the campaign, volunteer for the special event. Go ahead, give it the time. Let your candle burn at both ends if necessary. It will provide a dazzling light, a beacon for others to follow. And your own life will be extended in so many ways.

My candle burns at both ends.
It will last the entire night.
And ah, my friends, do note—
It gives a glorious light.

(With apologies to Edna St. Vincent-Millay for considerable tampering!)

46

IT IS SO SIMPLE

Ashley Hale is one of the great doyens in the field, a masterful consultant to the nonprofit world. A curmudgeon into his 80s, he continues to serve and to write and to remain one of the brilliant spokesmen in the business.

The other day, I was reading some material he prepared thirty years ago. I was struck with two elements I consider extraordinary.

First of all, the material was written three decades ago and it occurs to me—nothing has changed. Absolutely nothing.

And secondly, it seems so simple and easy to understand. Why is it, then, that trustees so often leave their role of governance and begin meddling in the operation of the institution. I know—and I'll write about this in a moment. But first, let me explain Ashley Hale's seven basic elements of institutional governance. Keep in mind that all of the following require a cooperative staff which, while assisting the board on the following matters, recognizes that the board is the final authority.

1. DEFINITION. Only the board can officially define the nature and purpose of the organization. Only the board can change the charter. Only the board can define the statement of the organization's mission.

2. GOALS. Only the board can officially establish institutional goals.

3. BUDGETS. Only the board can authorize annual operating budgets and major capital expenditures.

4. FINANCING. Only the board has ultimate responsibility for seeing that funds are made available to achieve official goals. The board oversees the budget and makes certain that it is balanced.

5. APPOINTMENTS. Only the board can hire and fire the chief executive officer. In many situations, but not all, the board also has the authority to confirm senior staff appointments, promotions, and tenure.

6. TRUST. Only the board can discharge the fiduciary responsibilities of the organization. It is the board's burden to see to it that the organization's assets are effectively managed in the public interest, in accord with the law, in keeping with the expectancy of the constituency, and the wishes of the donors.

7. ADVOCACY. The board has ultimate responsibility to see that the nature, purpose, operations, and accom-

plishments of the organization are known, understood, and appreciated.

In all of the seven essentials, the board should act on the advice of the chief executive officer. If it cannot consistently act on the chief's advice and counsel, it should get a new chief—someone it can have more confidence in.

And that is why I am certain that trustees begin getting involved in operations. They lack confidence in their chief. When I talk with staff who complain about board members who keep crossing the line of proper function, I ask them if this is in actuality a signal that is being sent. Most often, it is not a lack of understanding the difference between staff and trustee functions. It is a lack of confidence in the staff.

It is so clear. And so simple. The responsibility to advise is that of the staff. The authority to decide is that of the board.

The board must listen, but it need not heed. The board is responsible for the wisdom of its decisions. At times, the decisions may be difficult—but there is never a question as to who is responsible!

It is the responsibility of the chief executive officer to see that things are done right. It is the responsibility of the board to see that the right things are done.

And now you see how very simple it is. So don't muck it up!

47

EXTEND YOUR LEASE

I READ THE OTHER day of a most extraordinary departure on the part of one Foundation and its grants-making. Extraordinary, and with great merit.

The Ohio Higher Education Foundation has added a question to its application for grants that inquires about the amount of time trustees give to the board and to the organization. The amount of time! And it asks, also, how much money trustees give and get.

How would your board measure up with this Foundation?

The Ohio Higher Education Foundation is the creature of Leslie Wexner, who contributed $250 million to create it. Wexner believes that trustees need to be held to a higher standard of accountability and responsibility. Just attending meetings, lending your name, or giving lip service—that's not enough. Not nearly enough.

Almost all major national foundations do raise the question of how much board members are giving to support the organization or a specific project. But not all ask it quite as specifically as Wexner's group. Incidentally, I have never known of a case where a foundation worries about the amount of dollars trustees give. They are concerned only about 100 percent participation and giving to whatever level tests the capacity of trustees.

Wexner has some other principles worth noting. He doesn't believe in giving 'until it hurts.' His measure of successful giving is: "When I make a gift, do I really feel terrific? If I don't feel terrific, I know I haven't given enough."

How terrific do you feel?

Mr. Wexner wants to give and serve in a way that makes a difference. He says that you never know when your lease expires. I like his way of putting it. When we come into this life, we don't really own anything, and we own nothing when we leave. It is only a lease we have, and during each lifetime it is up to us to make the most of it.

"I'd like to feel that I've always met my obligations," Wexner says—"personal ones and community ones. I'd like to check out with 10 cents and see the good I've done while on earth."

I believe firmly that by giving and serving, working for others, by helping a mighty and worthy cause—you help extend your lease.

48

HOW LONG?

I N THE RESEARCH WE have done, I find that two hours is considered by trustees to be the maximum time they feel is necessary to spend at a board meeting. This is what trustees report to me. In actual practice, I find that they are willing to go even longer if it is an important session where consequential items are being discussed.

The exception to the two–hour rule, of course, is a college or university, or a national organization, where trustees come from great distances. Another exception would be an institution that has meetings quarterly or less frequently than that. In these situations, the meetings can profitably extend to a day or even two.

My experience is that two hours should be considered a maximum amount of time for most meetings. I have sat through my share of sessions that have gone on and on into the night—as they say, drawing straight lines from unwarranted assumptions to forgone conclusions. This almost never happens with a really effective board.

The necessary prescription is almost always a better prepared and more defined agenda, and a Chair who understands and has reviewed the agenda well in advance. The rambling meeting is also often a result of taking too much time with the unimportant.

I was at a board meeting of a YMCA in a small Michigan community. The session had gone on for three hours, and most of the time had actually been taken up with discussing how much members should be charged for the use of lockers and towels. No, I'm not kidding. There was heated debate on the issue, and it was finally left unresolved, to be discussed again at next month's meeting.

After three hours of haggling over lockers and towels, trustees were now ready to discuss an item that was of such immense consequence it could determine the future of the YMCA for the next few years and for a generation to come. But by this time, the group was exhausted. I don't blame them. I was, too. They started drifting away. About ten minutes into this crucial discussion, there were not enough trustees for a quorum.

You must savagely guard against what Goethe calls: "Things which matter most must never be at the mercy of things which matter least." That is an admonition which should be capitalized and underlined at the top of every board agenda.

49

COUNT PEOPLE, NOT NUMBERS

B E CONTINUALLY VIGILANT. Great ventures start with a vision and a dream, driven by a zeal of missionary proportions. And they often end with the rigidity of an iron structure.

You find it in every field, in every type of organization and institution. The loss of mission and focus is a clear case of the triumph of calcification over spirit. Too often, the bottom line, statistics, and volume dominate an organization's priorities. The investment of funds becomes more important than the investment in people.

When this happens, you're in trouble.

What may have begun as a phalanx of dreamers, sharing a singleness of purpose and faith, and seeking a declared destiny—becomes smothered in statistics, computer printouts, and organizational net worth. The number-people have won out.

Numbers are nice to count. But people are what really count.

50

THE BIG NINE

TO BE TRULY EFFECTIVE, a board cannot count on a few superstars. There must be a total team effort and the striving for group achievement. It's the work and effort of the total group that has meaning. When all work together, the synergism that takes place is invincible.

But it requires discipline in elephantine proportions, and determined and undistracted will power.

For some trustees, this call for discipline conjures up images of sacrifice and denial. This need not be the case at all, for in the joyous pursuit of an objective, there is the thrill and exhilaration of crossing new thresholds once thought unachievable.

Working together, sharing a common high purpose, it is possible for the board to be single-minded in its pursuit, and undeviating in its high expectation. No board meeting passes without a review and assessment, and renewed determination.

With a dedication to achieve, you will win great victories. You will be successful. You can count on it. But there is a price. You must make the effort. You must be unflinching in your determination until you achieve your objective.

Nine characteristics are common to a board that is motivated and disciplined.

1. There is an unswerving dedication to institutional purpose. You determine your objectives and you go for it. You commit the resources of the board and the organization to achieving the objective. You make certain there is the appropriate allocation of staff time and funds. You know what you want and you have a healthy dissatisfaction with anything less. Reaching your goal is so important to the work and success of the organization, each trustee can feel and sense the need.

2. Your objective becomes a matter of regular discussion and review at each board meeting. You concentrate on your promise. You demonstrate a devotion to your goal. You savor it. You discuss how it can achieve the great vision for your organization. It burns like fire in your bones.

It doesn't seem possible that anything as elusive and sensory as this type of group dynamics could possibly help determine the success of a program. I assure you it does. W. Clement Stone, the great Chicago philanthropist says: "If you can conceive it, you can achieve it." He believes unequivocally in this philosophy. So do I.

Stone, by the way, was captured by the vision of what could happen to a remote Michigan campsite if it were properly lead and funded. He was enthralled with the thought of making Interlochen a world-esteemed center for bright and talented young musicians. He joined their board, became its Chair, and gave extraordinary proportions of his time and money to make the dream a reality. He never once flagged in his determination, nor altered his course. The power of his resolve and will was infectious, and it carried everyone with him. He visualized his dream. He did indeed conceive it and achieve it.

3. The board is unafraid of failure. They certainly would not relish it, and they don't even expect it. In fact, the really disciplined and determined don't accept the meaning of the word. The board is intrepid, unconcerned about charting a new course, a new path. They never lose sight of their objective, but they understand it may require a new direction to get there.

4. The board is unshakable in its confidence. They know that the objective is sound, realistic, and relevant for their organization. But the timing and resources may require fine tuning.

5. They know it requires appropriate time to reach a worthy goal. But typically, the successful board does not demonstrate much understanding for patience. Most certainly, this would not be a trait considered one of its most redeeming features. In truth, there is almost always a healthy lack of patience.

6. Priorities and timelines are established. There is a plan of action, creatively conceived, time-phased, and rigorously pursued and implemented. There is a road map and from time to time, a detour may be required. But there is never any question about your final destination. Unlike the man on the Los Angeles freeway who says to his wife: "Don't worry honey that we're lost, we're making good time"—the disciplined board is never lost.

7. Proper resources are determined and understood. The disciplined board knows that great achievements require time, energy, appropriate staffing, and necessary funding. All these resources together can accomplish the extraordinary, the unthinkable.

8. Your persistence never waivers, never falters. Once de-

termined it is necessary for the institution's success, the objective is put on track and the goal-driven train is set in motion, powered by the dream, fueled by the conviction of the board.

There may be setbacks, disappointments, and struggle —but there is no let-up. There is only the will and the drive to carry forward, to reach new horizons, to achieve great things. You somehow succeed against impossible odds. Out of your courageous faith, there is this spark that ignites the proper motivation and inspiration. What a team! What a great victory! You are invincible.

9. You grow in strength and in resolve. There is a certain joy in the agony and the struggle to achieve great things. The board team becomes closer, united in a shared objective. There is excitement and exhilaration.

It requires hours and hours, meetings beyond meetings. But it is somehow worth the effort.

And then it happens. You achieve the impossible. You reach your objective. Every trustee is a champion. It could not have been done without the full and combined effort of all. And it could not have been done without rigid resolve and dogged determination.

I work with a fine independent school on the East Coast. For years, the board has discussed the need for new and added facilities. The school cannot maintain a quality program without the infusion of funds that would come from a larger student body. And this requires new facilities.

The board discusses this regularly. The project is one of their great wishes. But that's all it is—a wish.

There has never been the resolve and the determination to make it happen. "Gee, I wish we could have more classrooms." That's as far as the board gets.

No resolve, no will, no discipline. No classrooms.

51

GETTING THERE

E VEN IN HIS DAY, Lewis Carroll seemed to understand the concept of planning. His dialogue between Alice and the Cheshire Cat says it all.

"Would you tell me, please, which way I ought to go from here?" asked Alice.

"That depends a good deal on where you want to get to," said the cat.

"I don't much care where..." said Alice.

"Then it doesn't matter which way you go," said the cat.

Life was once easier. No longer! Life was more dependable. You could count on what to expect. No more.

Not too long ago, technology and social order could be trusted to stay carefully and quietly moored in place over long periods. But now, we live in a time of unparalleled change, disorder, and movement. You can be certain that when something has been done a particular way in your organization a few years or so, it is a good sign, in these changing times, that it is being done the wrong way. Or that others are doing it better.

For the organization dedicated to growth and development, there can only be one answer. Strategic and creative planning. And that is a responsibility of the trustees. It is achieved in a spirit and association of intimate coordination and harmony with the staff.

You have no choice but to anticipate the future. In today's explosive and frenzied race, planning becomes an absolute essential.

It's immensely confounding and challenging, the future-setting and strategic posturing of an organization. Niels Bohr, the Danish scientist, once said: "Forecasting is difficult and at times impossible—especially when it's about the future!"

Effective planning is a highly complex and puzzling riddle. There are new markets, different concepts, more aggressive competition. And more people to serve. Greater needs. New ways of doing things.

The fight for survival can be ferocious.

Without proper planning, an organization is without rudder or direction. The time finally comes to every organization when it must plan or perish.

Strategic planning is innovative, exploratory, venturesome, and visionary. Impatient with convention, the success-driven organization is attracted by the unknown and the undetermined. There must be a declaration of an overriding goal to greatness.

Proper planning determines the basic character of your organization—its mission and its vitality.

Planning is your lifeline. There must be a commitment to change, a fervor for boldness, and a determination to implement. Note this well: As a trustee, planning and an undaunting resolve to succeed can make the most audacious of dreams come true.

There was never a greater opportunity—for the organization which plans. Forceful, courageous, and imaginative plans. It means being driven by a single impulse and a predisposition to evaluate before acting. And then, the daring determination to act.

For your organization, there are new frontiers to conquer. If you do not truly believe this, prepare for the worst: The parade may pass you by. There are changing markets to serve. Men and women, families, young people who need your services. New objectives to be achieved.

Success is waiting, waiting for the organization responsive to unprecedented opportunities still unknown.

On the part of trustees, working with the staff, planning requires a disciplined effort, and an eagerness to be bombarded and challenged with questions: What else? Why not? Who says? Why must it be done this way?

Strategic planning helps you establish objectives. Determine policies. It empowers you to make the hard decisions. And it gives the insight to generate new and relevant ideas. And most of all, the dedication to translate these ideas into desired action. Where there is no bold vision and creative planning, the organization stands still. And in today's world of change, at times frantically and frighteningly fast, standing still could relegate you to an unquestionable second place

Or worse.

Are you a believer, as I am, in the glorious world of Dr.

Seuss. He understands all there is to know about strategic
planning:

"You can get so confused
That you'll start into the race
Down long wiggled roads at a break-necking pace
And grind on for miles across weirdish wild space,
Headed, I fear, toward a most useless place."

52

WHO SHOULD CALL

" PEOPLE GIVE TO PEOPLE." You hear the phrase so often. It is one of the glorious, revered laws of fundraising. The problem is, it isn't necessarily so.

People don't give to people. People give to the right person. And don't forget it!

As a matter of fact, the evidence seems quite clear that no matter how devastatingly powerful the leverage might be, no matter how close the relationship, even if the friendship is abiding and one of deep regard and affection—a donor will not make a really large gift to an institution he does not care about, no matter who makes the call.

The validation and data are overwhelming: People give their talent and their tithe when they believe in the mission of the institution. There is no other reason as significant or compelling.

Jack Whitehead is one of the major philanthropists in

the nation. He said to me: "I don't care who calls on me. There isn't enough leverage in the world that could make me give a major donation to a project I'm not interested in. Oh, I suppose if a very close friend or an important business colleague asked me for help, I would do something. But it certainly wouldn't be very much—and most likely, nothing. I need to be excited about the project. I need to feel that it's something I really care about. That's what really gets my money."

Marianne McDonald says she can tell if it's something she wants to give to in a major way because she can feel the vibrations in her bones.

People don't give to people. They give to great causes and they give to the magic of a compelling and dramatic idea. Marianne McDonald told me: "All I want to do with my life and my funds is to change the world. That's all!" That's how most donors feel. It's got to burn like fire in their bones, and it doesn't matter who makes the call.

But people give appointments to people, the right people. The leverage counts in getting the appointment, and that's no small matter. I am convinced that it's easier to get the gift than it is to get the appointment. Get your right people in the organization to make the appointment.

There's something even more significant. The concept comes from a small volume, written by James Gregory Lord. Donors don't give because your organization has needs. Every organization can use more money.

As a matter of fact, organizations do not have needs. People have needs, people have problems. Your organization has the answer, the solution.

People have needs. You have the response, the solution. So don't sell the need, sell the solution.

Buck Rogers was executive vice president of IBM over a

long period of the company's highest growth. He said: "At IBM, we don't sell equipment. We sell solutions." And that's it—sell the solutions your organization offers.

People don't give to people. They give to great crusades, magnificent causes, glorious and dazzling programs. They give to solutions.

53

BE SELECTIVE

JAMES WOLFENSOHN SAYS: "In order to be a good board member, it takes passion, caring, time, sacrifice."

Wolfensohn ought to know what he's talking about. He is Chairman of the board of the prestigious Institute for Advanced Study in Princeton, and Trustee of the Brookings Institution, Howard Hughes Medical Institute, and the Rockefeller University. A pretty significant collection!

But what has added to his woes recently is that he is currently the Chair of the board of trustees of both the Carnegie Hall in New York and the John F. Kennedy Center for the Performing Arts in Washington.

He says: "I am really tired. This is awful." He feels like he is on a fast slippery track, and indeed he is. He can't stop running. The problem is that he is a perfectionist and a detail person, mixed with a pretty healthy ego, and feels that any organization in which he is involved has to be run

" . . . as a business. You get judged by donors on whether you can manage it well."

The question is: How many boards can one person effectively serve?

In the case of Wolfensohn, his has been no modest achievement. When he became Chair of Carnegie Hall in 1980, the magnificent historic structure was coming apart at the seams. The board could not decide whether to fix it up or tear it down. They had pretty much decided to sell it when Wolfensohn entered the scene. He is the one who nagged the board to move forward on a campaign. Initially, it was determined that it would require $30 million to renovate the old lady. Through Wolfensohn's great effort, $60 million was raised for the stately landmark.

He says that all of his work at Carnegie Hall was a labor of love. But some describe his chairmanship as a combination of a wrecking ball and a flame thrower. Fan or not, everyone agrees that Wolfensohn brings a glorious mixture of connections, artful guile, and money. All in monumental proportions.

How does he do it all? How does he find the time? Well, some say he doesn't have the time to do it all effectively and that he is stretched too thin. More than that, there are a number who feel there is an enormous conflict of interest between his chairmanship at Carnegie Hall and the Kennedy Center.

How much can one person do, and how much should a person take on?

I was talking a year or two ago with the Vice President for Community Affairs of the major utility in Birmingham, Alabama. He was telling me how heavily involved he was in community activities and pulled out a sheet from his top desk drawer. On it were listed fourteen organizations and agencies in Birmingham where he sat on the board. I use the word "sat" advisedly!

Everyone understands that his job as vice president of the utility was to be the contact person for his company with the community. But how could he possibly serve that many organizations effectively? If it is true that a board member must bring concern and compassion to their trusteeship, and a not modest measure of passion and advocacy —how far can this be spread?

With all of the people I interviewed, Wolfensohn a notable exception, there was a feeling that you could not serve effectively on more than four or five nonprofit boards at the same time. And that would be the very most: A person who serves on too many boards makes me think of a stone skipping on a pond—taking a moment here and there to attend one meeting and ricocheting to the next. These trustees cover a lot of water, but only skim the surface. Just like the Platte River—a mile wide but only four inches deep.

Most often what I hear from people is that they are cutting back: "I allowed myself to get too involved. I said 'yes' to everyone and everything, and ended up not doing anything for anyone. I couldn't make meetings, and I couldn't make calls. Who needs a board member like that. And most of all, I was embarrassed. I think a person ought to take on an assignment only if they can give it the time and plan on doing a good job."

So here's the answer: Take on as many trusteeships as you feel you can handle effectively and with optimum results. For most people, four or five would be the very most. Just keep in mind that to meet the criteria for being effective, your attendance must be high, you must do your homework in preparing for meetings, your involvement must be sterling, you must be a rousing advocate, and you must be diligently and actively involved in organizational activities. And, oh yes—you must give generously and work assiduously at getting others to do the same.

And on top of all of that, it is important to avoid any conflict where there might be a overlapping or duplication of constituencies.

Be selective.

54

RECHARGING BATTERIES

TO TAKE A TRUSTEE'S dedication for granted, is to lose it. It must be sought and fought for. And it is worthy of the battle. An unswerving devotion to the cause must be nurtured and honed, with vigilance and doggedness. It must be hard-fought and rewon at every board meeting, throughout the trustee's tenure, and beyond.

In today's world, it is not always easy to maintain a trustee's ardor. There are time demands and other activities. And there is an insatiable search for the most influential and talented leadership possible—other organizations covet your best trustee material. The competition for the effective trustee is fierce and others vie with you for the best leadership.

On occasion, a trustee's enthusiasm will wane and weaken. This should underline the importance for you to have a program to keep your valued trustees galvanized to the cause. This imposes a grave responsibility on the chief staff person and the chair to maintain each trustee's focus to what I call "the passion of the cause."

There are ways to keep the trustee's battery at a state of constant positive charge. One is to make certain that the agenda at each meeting provides for stimulating discussion and an opportunity for a major decision. Trustees must feel a sense of worth and importance to the organization.

A regular flow of information and communications is important. And don't overlook the opportunity for human interest stories for the trustees. Even board members need to be reminded on a regular basis how significant their involvement is to the cause and to the constituencies that are being served. In the end, the reason people serve is because they want to make a difference, they want to help change lives and save lives.

Trustee contacts and visits from the chief officer are important. This might involve a luncheon or just a brief session in the trustee's office. These few minutes pay handsomely.

This business of keeping trustees within the loop and on a continual cycle of highs and excitement—this is all imperative. There should be a plan that is designed and implemented by the chief and the chair. You will want to include an annual retreat, special forms of recognition, special ways to express appreciation.

What you hope for, but what you must never count on or assume—is that each trustee gives testimony to his or her faith in the organization. What you expect are trustees who profess a high sense of dedication. What Yeats describes as "full of passionate intensity."

This dedication may not be present at first, when a trustee is initially enlisted and during his or her early tenure. Perhaps that is too much to expect. But surely in time, it is not too much to hope for.

55

COUNT ON
CHANGE

IT WAS A LONG time ago that I went to high school. In the late 1940s, George Gallup had just completed a study to determine what were the top eight discipline problems in public schools. Read what was considered really serious at that time: Talking, chewing gum, making noise, running in the halls, getting out of turn in line, wearing improper clothes, not putting paper in wastebaskets, going down the "up" stairs.

A survey just conducted this past year lists these top problems: drug abuse, alcohol abuse, pregnancy, suicide, rape, robbery, assault, and gang warfare.

Change is inevitable, but today it is taking place at an accelerated pace that is frightening. Social agendas have been re-ordered. New distortions are profound and far-reaching. The mind can hardly fathom all the implications.

Chicago provides a disturbing example. But it is by no

means an exception. Every major city faces the same crisis. Smaller communities, too.

In one Chicago high school, there is day care for the children of the high school students, 90 percent of whom come from public housing. There is another school where a 14-year-old is in her third pregnancy.

The *Chicago Tribune* reports: "One student sleeps with five other children on three piled-up mattresses in an unheated apartment. During the winter, the boy often came to school smelling of urine because it was too cold for the smaller kids to get up and go to the bathroom at night."

What is society's response to today's social trauma? What is happening affects every facet of life, every type of institution. In one way or another, it has impact on yours.

No matter what your institution—a college, a hospital, a social agency, whatever—if you are still providing service today as you did yesterday, you are not doing what needs to be done. You are not coping with the change that is taking place all about you.

None of this is really new. In the Garden of Eden, Adam paused at one point and said: "Eve, I believe we are going to be living in a time of great change." The only stability that is predictable is the stability in constant change.

Count on change. Plan on it.

56

HOW TO FAIL

RECENTLY, WE CONDUCTED A study for a New England college. The man who heads the board has been Chair for the past half dozen years. He is a successful businessman, a recognized leader, and a person of some affluence. When we asked how much he would give to the proposed major campaign for endowment, he said: "I'm not going to give. I think endowment spoils an institution."

Now that's the sort of thing that can cause severe palpitations, and no little stress, in a college president!

Trustees tend to follow the lead of the Chair. An axiom you can pretty well count on is that the pace and the enthusiasm of the Chair determines the pace and enthusiasm of the board. You can be certain in your projection of the college I described, because of the Chair's apathy, and indeed negativism—the board will follow suit. The project is moribund. This small college that desperately needs an endowment to undergird its truly fine program will have to wait. Wait, for a better time or a more dedicated Chair.

A great organization must have a sense of destiny. On the part of the Chair and trustees, there must be a willingness that knows no bounds. In the case of this small college, there will be a period of demoralization, then decline, and then totally deterioration—and it started with the Chair's apathy, rigidity, and vision starvation. In all likelihood, there was no great commitment to begin with.

Trustees must be willing to give. This is what transforms vision into reality. If those who are closest to you do not donate, it is a serious failure, a decaying of moral fortitude, determination, and dedication.

Now compare the example of the small northeastern college I described with the University of New England. UNE is less than thirty years old, practically a state of infancy in this country for private universities. It has a medical school, the only one in the State of Maine. It has a president who is willing to call on anyone and a senior development officer who is experienced and savvy. It's quite a combination.

Jean Wilkinson heads this energetic institution. As Chair, she leads with a very light and caring touch. But there is a will and a determination of tempered steel. She knows exactly where she's going and where she hopes to take the institution.

I asked her if the question of giving is discussed when the University of New England recruits new men and women to its board.

"You bet. When we ask someone to serve with us, we want them to feel it's something special, an honor. But we make it very clear that we expect them to call on others for gifts and we expect them to give. One hundred percent of our board gives, and while it is not stated in our by-laws that this is necessary, it would be unthinkable to me that we wouldn't have full participation.

"Why would a person serve on a board if they were not

planning on giving? Certainly a person understands that being asked to join a group like ours means they will be asked and will be expected to make a gift. We're so young and working so hard, and developing so fast, and coming up with such exciting ideas—we need all of the gifts we can get. And it has to start with our board.

"And I expect trustees to give sacrificially. By that, I mean that they should give as much as they possibly can. I want them to really stretch. If they are on the boards of other organizations and this dilutes their power of giving, perhaps they are on too many boards. They ought to make a decision."

When Jean Wilkinson speaks of sacrifice, I'm certain she means something more significant than Artemus Ward's: "I have already given two cousins to the war, and I stand ready to sacrifice my wife's brother."

Giving starts with the board. Great things happen when trustees are committed to a program of giving that is thoughtful and sacrificial. St. Matthew said that where your treasure is, there will your heart be, also. Even in that time, the power of giving was understood.

Guess which institution has the greatest potential for growing and flourishing—that northeastern college I described with the apathetic Chair, or the University of New England. I hardly need ask. UNE has a rendezvous with destiny, and while their finances will be a problem short-run, their future is exceedingly bright.

Peter F. Drucker is one of the most significant voices today in management and organizational structure. He has just written a superb book for nonprofits and it should be considered required reading. It is listed in the Bibliography.

He points out that the first constituency in fund development at any institution is its own board.

Drucker says it is no longer enough that a board simply be in sympathy with the institution—that represents a characterization of what he calls the old-type board. "You need a board that takes an active lead in raising money, whose members give both of themselves and by being fundraisers ... When a board member calls and says, 'I am on the board of the hospital,' the first response he gets from his friend is, 'How much are you giving yourself.'"

Drucker says that if the response is five hundred dollars from the trustee—well, that's about what you are likely to get from the other fellow.

Trustees who do not give, place their institution in manacles—forged and fashioned of a rigid spirit and lowly aspirations. The vision of the institution perishes. In an institution where trustee giving is not whole-hearted and understood—efficiency takes precedence over enthusiasm, the bottom-line wins out over service, and numbers become more important than mission.

It is a mysterious thing. At times, almost magical. It's hard to know what makes it all happen and why it seems to work so well.

You bring fifteen or twenty-five men and women together and they spend a lot of time they don't have.

At times they argue and fight.

They give money for a variety of programs, and even buy raffles, and sponsor tables at special events. Even though they might not like doing it, they ask their best friends for a gift. And to their amazement, they give more themselves than they ever thought possible.

Out of all of this comes dazzling achievements.

The organization does a magnificent job. The momentum is exhilarating. Hundreds are served in consequential ways. There isn't even time to ask: "Who the devil talked me into becoming a trustee in the first place?"

57

WHEN TO STOP

D AN GUSTINA HAS CHAIRED just about every organization in Eugene, Oregon. And he has lead or been
heavily involved in every capital campaign in that community in the past twenty years. He was also the senior volunteer and Chairman of the Foundation at Oregon State
University, his alma mater. In terms of volunteerism and
fundraising, there's very little that Dan Gustina hasn't
done!

He lives in Eugene but spends as much time at his second home in Indian Wells, California. There, he has three
country clubs he belongs to where he can play at his great
passion. And he's no novice. This past year, he won the
club championship at the El Dorado Country Club in the
desert.

He's now 73 and by anyone's measure, he...well, as
they say in Eugene, he's comfortable! He's at an age when
he could be doing just about anything he wants to. And he

could be spending more time on the golf course and relaxing. He has certainly earned that time.

Then why does he continue to be extremely active in community affairs in Eugene. And serve on the board of the Health and Hospital Services of the Sisters of St. Joseph of Peace. They have ten meetings or so a year in Seattle, and that means at least a couple days just about every month he travels from his home in the desert to Seattle. Why does he do it? He's paid his dues and his reputation would not suffer if he dropped off this board.

"I continue to serve on that board because I feel it is something where I can make a real contribution. I believe I bring a talent for business and good judgment. It's my way of repaying the good fortune that I have received. It's something I feel I just must do. There are times when a meeting conflicts with something special or important that is personal and I would perhaps enjoy doing more. But that's part of giving back, also."

58

WHAT REALLY COUNTS

I MET RECENTLY WITH fifty-three men and women who are chief executive officers of the Easter Seals Society. These are the professionals who head the largest chapters in the country. Great people. Bright, effective, and eager to succeed.

We got to talking about how they spend their time. I had them put some figures down on a pad and turn them in to me. It was disheartening, but not totally surprising.

Almost all spend 2 percent of their time or less in trustee development. And they spend even less time than that on board recruitment.

How do these fine executives spend their time? This won't surprise you either. Administration comes first, as you would expect. Next comes meetings—with staff and volunteers. All kinds of meetings. For some, it amounted to as high as fifty percent of their time.

This encouraged one of the chapter execs to say that

these meetings bring together a collection of individuals who separately do nothing and together decide that nothing can be done. The unfit, trying to lead the unwilling, to do the unnecessary!

Small wonder an organization often has a board less strong than it should be or merits. Assisting in the recruiting of board members is a function of the chief executive officer. It is a responsibility of consequential proportions. When handled effectively, the executive assists in suggesting names and acts as a consultant to the committee responsible for recruiting.

The style and character of the board tends to follow and represent the personality and pace of the chief executive officer. The stronger the staff person, the stronger the board. A powerful and inspiring executive attracts powerful and exciting trustees.

I have been at this business so long that I can almost determine after only a brief visit at a board meeting what caliber of trustees are involved. When there is a weak board, you can almost be certain that there is a weak executive.

It is my own strong bias that the chief executive officer should be a vocal, visible, and a contributing member of the Committee on Trusteeship. You will recall that I described earlier that this is the group that meets every month to discuss and evaluate present trustees and suggest names for future enlistment. The executive should have a major presence at these meetings, perhaps the primary one, but should not vote. The executive acts as a consultant—to recommend names and respond to questions.

It is not easy these days, recruiting the most effective board members possible for the organization. There are over one million nonprofits, and the competition for dedicated trustees is fierce. Getting the right board member is often a series of disappointments with a pleasant surprise here and there. I think it was Woody Allen who said something such as: "Getting good board members is just about as tough as getting a plumber on a weekend!"

This underlines the transcendent importance of spending the necessary time in the search and enlistment process —and in this regard, the executive officer plays one of the most important roles.

My experience with the Easter Seal executives is almost certainly no different than what I would have found with any other organization. As a matter of fact, I had almost precisely the same response from a larger group of United Way executives.

If it is true—and it is—that the board of an organization determines the program and services, the funding, and the vitality of the institution, you need the strongest board possible. If it is true—and again it is—that the board determines the destiny of the organization, you need the strongest and most effective trustees possible. This being the case, it is difficult to explain why so little time is given to such a precious imperative.

It is not enough for an executive to do things right. They must do the right things. And most consequential among these right things is having the strongest board possible.

The most effective executives I have worked with are tree-shakers and trustee-makers. Even if it means fewer meetings. They spend more time on board development— present and future. And it pays.

A chief executive usually gets the caliber of board he or she deserves.

GUESS WHAT TOPS
THE LIST

E VEN THOUGH IT WAS fifteen years ago, I can remember the day as if it were yesterday. We were having a meeting of the Cabinet for the YMCA campaign in San Diego. Malin Burnham was Chair of the Cabinet.

He told the group that we were going to have to ask the Chair of the campaign to resign. More than that, we were going to have to ask him to remove his name from anything at all to do with the YMCA. And even more than that—Malin didn't feel we could accept this person's gift.

There were horrible disclosures which were about to be released that only a very few in San Diego knew about—and Malin, being one of the very major leaders in the city, was close to what was going on. He told us that when the news broke, it would be devastating.

I felt sunk. I don't mind saying that I worked awfully hard to get that gift in the first place. And we worked twice as hard to get this person's commitment for leadership. I didn't feel very inclined to give it all up. Not that easily.

And the Cabinet was split, also. The person we were talking about, he was a model in the community—one of San Diego's leading and most visible citizens. At one point, he was named Man of the Year. Soon after that, he was named Man of the Mid-Century. This was no small matter we were discussing.

"Arnie has to go," said Malin. "There can be no wavering on this issue. It's a matter of our integrity and the integrity of the YMCA. Of course, we all need to show him personally our compassion and charity, but that can't get in the way of the only decision we can make. I'll tell him myself." And he did! And we recruited a new Chair.

Integrity cannot be bought and it cannot be measured in money. The best public relations consultant in the world can't acquire it for you. And fancy slogans and promises for the future won't help.

There can be no twilight zone. Something is either right or wrong, black or white. Because it must be a requisite of board membership, it determines the fiber and character of the organization.

In an organization, integrity must permeate every aspect of its activity. It demands a singleness of purpose, purged of compromise or the search for a material or program gain. Some objectives change continually, sometimes overnight. But the integrity of an organization does not change with time, or mood, or because of circumstances. In every case, it is personalized by the leadership—the staff and the trustees.

It means telling it as it is. Always. It means reflecting the highest principles. Always. There must be a devotion to what is right and honest and just.

The measure of a great organization is not recorded in its volume, its activities, or its growth—although all of these are important. But growth can change, flow and ebb with the tides of time. Integrity requires the stamina, the resourcefulness, and the daring of leadership. With it, an organization can accomplish all things.

Morals. Ethics. Standards. Integrity. From these flow a torrent of values. Deeds, not words. It is a clear case of what trustees do that speaks with such deafening impact. It is not what they say they do that counts—it is what they actually do.

I recently conducted a study to determine what is deemed to be a trustee's most important traits and characteristics. What quality is the most significant, I asked. Integrity led the list. No other attribute was close.

Honesty in a trustee and in the organization isn't the best policy. It is the only policy. There are times when the questions come faster than the answers. When the situation is complex, a total riddle. When there might be less travail to take the easier road. For an individual and an organization it can be a rigorous test. But integrity isn't a sometimes thing for a trustee. It is everything.

Earlier, in several sections, I wrote about the importance of trustees who should bring the three Ws to the board and their organization—Work, Wisdom, and Wealth. I feel that formula remains relevant and appropriate, but I suggest an alternative that is even more encompassing. I call it the *THE FIVE Is:* Integrity, Intelligence, Involvement, Investment, and Influence. I thought this said it all.

But Gary Strack has a list of his own *Is* that he looks for in his trustees. Gary is CEO and president of the Orlando Regional Medical Center in Florida. It is generally conceeded that Gary has one of the most effective and influential boards in the area. He really works at the recruiting process. He wants the best trustees he can possibly enlist.

Gary's list was the same as mine, with two notable additions—both of which I consider highly acceptable. The first is Inthusiasm—which I find totally worthy, even with Gary's outrageous spelling in order to make my list! The second is Intestines. Gary feels that an effective trustee needs the guts to make bold decisions.

And here it is, a list of seven criteria that is about as inclusive as you can make it. There is really nothing significant that is missing. This is your quick guide to measure your present board and future trustees.

THE SEVEN Is

INTEGRITY	inflexible and unyielding
INTELLIGENCE	wise decisions and good judgement
INVESTMENT	a willing and sacrificial giver
INFLUENCE	high visibility and regard
INTESTINES	ready to make tough decisions
INVOLVEMENT	active and hearty
INTHUSIASM	a constant and zealous advocate

And you'll note—INTEGRITY leads the list.

60

WHERE ARE
YOU GOING?

I N 1917, JULIUS ROSENWALD provided the funds for one of
the largest and most significant foundations of its time.
Mr. Rosenwald was a founder of Sears, Roebuck & Co.,
and amassed a fortune. What was remarkable about the
gift was that it was Mr. Rosenwald's unalterable wish that
the Foundation go out of business.

During its time, the Foundation was renowned for its work
with blacks. It was the forerunner of all else in this field. In
1948, with all of its achievements and great work, it closed its
doors. It gave away all its money. It consumed its endowment, precisely in accord with Rosenwald's wishes.

Mr. Rosenwald's view was that a permanent endowment
was bound to be one of continuing disappointment and de-
creasing vitality. He once wrote: "The history of charities
abounds in illustrations of the paradoxical axiom that while
charity tends to do good, perpetual charities tend to do
evil."

Right on!

This wise man, Julius Rosenwald, was saying that social agendas and human imperatives change. Because of these ever-altering conditions, a donor's original hopes and expectations would become obsolete, perhaps even counterproductive, if they were allowed to remain as originally constituted. He also felt the tendency for what is done in perpetuity can so easily be surrounded by a circle of trepidity.

It is the same with institutions. Those that show the greatest concern for conserving capital and maintaining a hoary, unchallenged mission—have the greatest chance of losing it all. An overstuffed, fat, self-satisfied organization is the greatest deterrent to a dynamic, flexible, and ever-renewing program.

The California Historical Society was in serious trouble. For them, it was one minute to midnight, a breath away from bankruptcy. The media was relentless in their coverage of the alleged poor management of the organization and the weak, uncommitted board. That was a year ago, but the media is still unabating.

Here's what caused the near-demise of this great organization. It wasn't the only reason, but it was indeed a major element. The Society was headquartered in a gorgeous mansion, vintage of the old barons, in Pacific Heights in San Francisco. Pacific Heights is considered the area of greatest concentrated wealth in the world. All of the efforts of the Society, all of its energy and dedication, were directed to the maintenance of that dazzling old mansion.

And that was the problem. Cheryl Kolinen puts it perfectly. She is the Director of Development of the Society. She says: "There was too much attention to the mansion. Too much mansion, and not enough mission."

It can happen when there is too much organization and structure. And not enough mission and ardor. Many institutions are guilty of building the church, and killing the creed.

There are organizations that are self-perpetuating, flabby, and rudderless. They are in direct odds with dynamic and growing institutions which the historian Daniel Boorstin characterizes as being spontaneous, fluid, and competitive.

It's so very easy to get your priorities askew.

A distinguished past is no assurance of your future. Lord Nesselrode was one of the greatest diplomats of his time. Today, he is immortalized as a pudding!

61

ADMIT YOUR BOARD

THE OTHER DAY, I was involved in a board retreat for the Medical Center in St. Helena, California. It's important for a group of trustees to get away, and be able to have the luxury of a full day, unhurried, to discuss the work, future, and vision of the institution. With this particular group, it was exciting and invigorating. They are really committed and rousing enthusiasts for the hospital.

Most people need to be reminded rather than informed. A carefully planned retreat is an extraordinary opportunity to do both.

It occurred to me early, however, that trustees did not really have much depth of information or understanding about the hospital. And the more we talked, I believe that they felt this, also.

I don't know about the restrictions and in today's world, you can't admit people willy-nilly into a hospital—but I suggested that each board member ought to spend an evening at the hospital. They could all be given a full physical examination—and in the process through Admissions, be assigned a room, and meet a number of the employees and nurses. I would not suggest that they all check in at the same time but, one by one, trustees could spend the evening and learn a great deal about their institution.

I can tell you that from the standpoint of a consultant, the best way I have of learning more about a hospital when we are doing a development audit, is to be admitted and spend the evening. It never fails. I learn a great deal about the maintenance of the facility and the morale of the staff. I learn first-hand about the food and the way patients are handled. It's the best way possible to strip back the layers of board reports and determine for yourself what makes the institution tick.

At Orlando Regional Medical Center in Florida, they have a program for trustees which merits replication in every hospital, and in every institution. At ORMC, each board member is expected to spend a full day at the hospital—to job-shadow a surgeon, a nurse, a radiologist, or any staff person of choice. The trustee decides where they want to spend the day. There are a dozen choices, such as the Trauma Center, open heart surgery, the MRI Center, or the Children's Hospital.

When the trustee arrives early in the morning, there's a staff person waiting—with full instructions and a schedule of the day's activities. There's also a gown with the trustee's name stitched on it. A magnificent touch! Often, there is time in the doctor's dining room for lunch. And then back to seeing patients.

Are trustees willing to give up a full day? You bet. It's considered one of the great benefits of serving on the board at ORMC. And, not incidentally, a masterful program for interpreting the work of the hospital and its staff, and a dramatic first-hand look at saving lives.

And if it works in hospitals, the same concept can be adapted to most other organizations. Think about how to put this to use for your board.

62

JUST FOR LOVE

YEARS AGO, COLONEL LOUIS WELLS was engaged to provide fundraising counsel for what was then called the
Dallas Community Chest. At the time, Lou Wells was just
about the most outstanding and effective consultant in the
business.

The Chair said: "Mr. Wells, you will be returning in about
two months to start your work for the Chest. Between now
and then, what can we do?" Lou thought for a moment and
then said: "Resign!" And he did. And many of the board
did. And it was the right thing. The Community Chest had
the wrong leadership to raise significant funds.

The trustees of an organization are a bunch of amateurs!
They are amateurs in the truest meaning of the word.

The word amateur has its roots from the Latin *amateur*—
full of love. And these trustees, this wonderful group of amateurs, they serve entirely for the love of the institution and
for its noble cause.

It's an awesome responsibility. These amateurs have unequivocal and final responsibility for the welfare and well-being of a million non-profit organizations. In their thoughtful and compassionate care, they guide and help fund the activities and programs which benefit millions and millions. The homeless, blood banks, battered women, the Scouts, character-building institutions, medical centers, food banks, colleges and universities, work for the disenfranchised, and more. Much more.

They give thousands and thousands of hours, these amateurs. And they do it willingly and selflessly, just for the love of it.

Alex de Tocqueville had a difficult time understanding it. "It is quite remarkable what these Americans do. They give their time and money to a host of organizations, and they do it willingly. There is nothing quite like it anywhere else in the world. I find it remarkable." That was written 160 years ago when the young Frenchman came to this country to try to discover what generated the extraordinary vitality that existed here in such abundant proportions. That same zeal and exuberance for helping others, just for the love of it, exists to this day.

Some would say that is what continues to make this nation the greatest in the world. It is this group of amateurs, an army estimated to be over 15 million.

An extraordinary person, the amateur trustee. Very often, he does not know what can't be done—and he is so dumb he will just go ahead and try it. And it will work!

This amateur will give selflessly of his time—hours and hours, weeks on end, one year after the other. And these amateurs, they will spend untold funds, dig very deep into sometimes shallow pockets, for those institutions that are close to their hearts and causes they love dearly.

It is said that God has very special affection for this extraordinary army of amateurs.

63

DEMAND MORE

RANDALL MEYER RECENTLY RETIRED as President of the Exxon Company. Over the years, he has served as a trustee of several dozen nonprofits—his alma mater, the University of Iowa; Methodist Hospital in Houston, one of the largest medical centers in the nation; The Kincaid School, where he serves as Chair; and M.D. Anderson, the premier cancer treatment center in the world. And more.

In his rise at Exxon, and during his presidency, he was as busy as any senior corporate executive could possibly be. The pace was frantic. The claim on his attention and energy, unending. But he still found time to serve as a trustee. "It's the way I pay back," says Meyer.

Randall Meyer feels keenly that too often trustees don't take their job seriously enough. "No one sits them down and says—'You have a fiduciary responsibility that you cannot escape. You have got to exercise stewardship on behalf of your organization.' "

The world makes way for the organization that knows where it's going. That's why Meyer says that every institution needs to pay attention to its planning process and activity. If it does not, it's unlikely that Meyer will be willing to continue to serve. "I guess it's my corporate background. In business, we are always planning ahead. If you don't, the parade will pass you by. But I think the same is true for the nonprofit. Perhaps even more so.

"I insist that any organization that I serve must have a strategic long-range plan. And if they don't, I want to help them in putting one together. The nonprofit that doesn't plan ahead will not be around in the future. And I don't want to serve on that kind of a board."

In a Gallup poll that was conducted recently, it was reported that men and women serve on boards because they really want to help people. That was the primary and overriding reason. Around the nation, men and women are linked as trustees, serving organizations in a variety of noble causes.

It is well to understand, however, that in addition to the great desire to help others, board members must accept the legal anticipation and responsibility that they are overseers of a public trust.

A public trust! This is a sacred commitment you make in accepting a trusteeship. Not to be taken casually, this responsibility. Randy Meyer says that the key to being an effective board member is not that you manage more—but that you demand more.

64

WHAT A TIME

THE FIRST DAY IT started raining, someone thought they heard Noah saying: "Lord, it looks like I'm living in a period of transition."

For this decade, and into the new century, there likely will not be a time without problems, trouble, and great complexity. It's life on the high wire, a minute 'til midnight.

It is also a time of unprecedented opportunities. For the organization that is willing to break through old barriers, to chart a new course, to envision great dreams and new hopes—there was never a time of greater promise and high expectations.

The board that protects its vested interest and its precious heritage has a tendency to block necessary change. The result can be, at best, stagnation. A stunted growth. At worse, paralysis and extremis.

A ho-hum board begets a ho-hum institution. Plain vanilla! No soaring hopes. No exciting aspirations. No creative solutions. An organization such as this will never be able to respond to human and social needs. As a trustee, it is your responsibility to be continuously vigilant—to review, package, and revitalize the program of your organization. If you don't, you are only treading water.

In today's environment, there is no allowance for complacency. For your organization, there is no longer a time without challenge.

A board that is apathetic has pre-determined that its institution will stagnate. A board that is uncommitted ensures an institution that is moribund.

Trustees must give sustenance and strength. Fervor and vitality. Courage and stamina. It takes all of this. If you don't have the will and the want, then ask yourself: "Why? Why am I serving?"

The opportunities were never greater. You may be exceedingly proud of your institution's sanctified founding and your rich heritage, but it is to the future that you must look for your most heroic achievements. You must be willing to consider untested and untrusted alternatives to your institution's time-tested and trusted practices.

If your organization is deeply rooted to its ways of the past, chances are almost certain that you are in trouble. The acceleration of change is unprecedented. It is perplexing to plan very far in the future. It is a dilemma to plan even for the present! A trustee must be dynamic, audacious of spirit, and prepared to leap for the opportunity. A board is no place for the too timid or the too tidy of mind.

What was good enough in yesterday's service will not be good enough today. You can count on that. And most certainly, it will not be good enough tomorrow. You can be sure of that. Tried and true must be continually tested as still-true.

For organizations, taking the safe way and the known

road, is certain defeat. Trustees who dare, who travel the unchartered, risk much—and gain everything.

What is important is that a trustee must have the freedom to break with tradition. And challenge cherished practices. Your organization may be on the very brink of greatness—waiting for you and other trustees to wage a lapel-grabbing iconoclastic evolution. A quiet revolution. A rebellion of rising expectations.

There was never a time when your organization was needed more. But not with yesterday's programs, or today's services. You face head-on opportunities, chilling concerns, roller coaster social agendas that are inextricably complex and in a constant state of change. The future belongs to the organization with soaring visions, unyielding faith, unlimited expectations, and commitment that never ends.

65

DON'T JUST SLASH EXPENSES

PROPER FUNDING AND FINANCIAL solvency is the responsibility of the board. And absolutely no one within the institution seems to object to that: "Let the board do it!" cheer all in emphatic and joyful unison!

That sobering thesis is one of the thrusts in a remarkable book called *"The Board and The President,"* by James L. Fisher. And Fisher should know what he writes about. He is a recognized authority on leadership and the author of several of the most celebrated books on governance in higher education. He was cited as being one of the outstanding university presidents in the nation, and for nearly ten years headed the Council for Advancement and Support of Education.

Fisher says that while just about everyone wants to run the institution—the faculty, the board, the students, the alumni, and the community—they all turn confidently (and thankfully) to the board for financial support.

It is the board's responsibility to see to it that income equals expenditures. If the revenue does exceed expenses, even by a bit—it does tend to provide a great comfort (and longer tenure!) to the chief executive officer, and eases the palpitations in the heart. When the finances are not in balance, it's up to the trustees to review the situation carefully, assess the conditions, and take appropriate steps.

You can balance the budget in two ways: By reducing your costs or by increasing the income. The latter is almost always the preferable way.

In a number of institutions, I have witnessed firsthand a board that collectively and corporately rolls up its sleeves and takes action. The wrong action! They slash away at expenses.

Certainly, trustees and staff alike abhor unnecessary expenses. But to cut staff, services, and activities very often leaves a much greater imbalance—a program and service deficit. With the program deficit, you have heard the first dull clang of the organizational death knoll.

Increase income. That's really the most appropriate solution and effective answer. Fisher says that in all of his experience, he has never seen a board that was not too involved in the financial affairs, and not sufficiently informed about the programs of the institution. I would add that very often a board is far too involved in the financial affairs of the institution, and not sufficiently or effectively involved in its fundraising needs.

There is some sort of a law, I firmly believe, that governs this phenomenon at board meetings. My experience is: The length of the material, the depth of the documentation, and the heat of the discussion—is in inverse proportion to the agenda item's importance to the future of the institution!

Fisher says that what is needed is a more creative view of

the problem and a more entrepreneurial approach. And more effective fundraising.

In today's world, the Peter Pan approach won't work— "Clap once if you hear Tinker Bell." It's a tough and realistic world out there, nothing like Never-Never Land. Trustees have a responsibility to review the operation carefully and to do whatever is necessary to ensure that there is neither a financial imbalance or a program deficit. Both render the institution impotent, and without vitality or proper service.

That's the rub. To balance the budget but operate a program and service deficit—is to abdicate your trusteeship.

66

GIVE YOUR
BUSINESS A LIFT

"THE MORE TIME I give to my volunteer work, the better my company does."

That's a pretty astounding statement but that was only the beginning.

George D. Behrakis and I were finishing a snack at the World Trade Center in Boston. We had just completed a successful call for a major gift, and George was in a pretty mellow mood. I didn't blame him. He had done a superb job on the call and was feeling ten feet tall!

George told me that he spends about twenty-five hours a week in his various trustee activities. He puts in another sixty hours a week in his company. That's two full weeks of work in one. He admits to being a workaholic. I could have guessed!

"I love it. I feel every activity I'm involved in is important. I really believe that I'm an excellent board member. I do my homework and I work hard. I believe I am helping mankind but down deep, I know that what I do for others is important to me personally."

George loves a challenge. "What I think I like most of all is becoming involved in an organization that's in trouble. I love the challenge. I love being able to get deeply involved and help turn things around.

"But what I can't explain is what happens when I take on some major time commitments. My business does better. It's been that way all my life. It's not rational but I find that the harder I work for others, the better I do for myself."

George Behrakis heads one of the largest pharmaceutical houses in the nation. He manages to balance a frantic travel schedule, including regular trips to Europe, with board memberships at his community hospital, Northeastern University, Hellenic College, the Boy Scouts, and the Archdiocesan Council of the Greek Orthodox Church of North and South America. That's his current list and on three, he has served as Chair.

George loves it and for him, the more he gives, the more he seems to get back.

I hear that same sort of thing from others. A dozen others. Take V.H. Van Horn for instance. Pete Van Horn is President of the National Convenience Stores. He was one of the very early ones that came up with the idea of those wonderful small stores that stock everything, are open day and night, and are often attached to gasoline stations. When he opened his convenience store, it was the first in the country. Since that time, his network has grown to be one of the largest in the nation.

Pete Van Horn has plenty to do, running his growing company, and overseeing its development in both quality and in revenue. He is still one of those who enjoys popping in to one of his stores to make certain that everything is in order and that high standards are maintained.

He takes time from his heavy business commitments to participate fully in community activities. Several years ago, he headed the United Way in Houston, and set an all-time high. United Way receives more per capita in Houston than in any city its size in the nation. He's also on the boards of a half dozen other organizations, and he gives them each a great deal of time.

What drives him to do this? "The city is our corporate headquarters and I feel it is important to give back time and money to the community. But I find it personally rewarding, also. I get a lift. I know what I do is important but it also means a lot to me personally."

"And you know," he said. "I think it's good business. I don't do it for that reason, but it somehow always seems to come back. It really does. I hate to even talk about this because it gives volunteering the wrong twist, but it does indeed come back."

As an example of what he says is the type of thing that happens often, he told me a story to prove his point. It happened three or four years ago. "I was vice-chairman of our Boy Scout Council and at one of our big annual dinners, I was asked to sit next to a fellow we were counting on for a very large gift. In the course of the evening, I did ask for the gift. But something else happened. This fellow had a store that he was eager to sell and we bought it and brought it into our network. It became one of our largest producers. Something like this always seems to happen. When I work hard for one of the organizations where I'm on the board, something good happens to me."

I could go on with stories just like this. I heard the same sort of thing from every trustee I interviewed. But Charles Miller said it best of all. He is President of the Transamerica Criterion Group—the largest team of investment counselors in the nation. He doesn't have time, but he makes it. He's on the board of St. John's College in Annapolis and Santa Fe, a host of cultural boards, and a member of the board of visitors of M.D. Anderson, one of the great cancer centers in the world. Recently, he has become particularly interested in some of the problems and concerns of the Hispanics, and has joined the board of several organizations which serve this group.

Why does he do it? Why does he give all those volunteer hours?

"I get involved because I get so much back. I'm not talking about helping my fellow man and doing good. Sure, I know that's true. But what I mean is, it's good for me. Do you understand—it's good for me. And it's fun."

But you, you're a trustee—and you already knew all of this. You know that the more you put into your volunteer work, the more you seem to get back. And it's fun.

But don't spread the word. Some would call you just plain selfish for doing so much good and enjoying it so immensely.

67

BE A GUARDIAN
OF THE VISION

TRUSTEES EXIST TO GOVERN an organization. It is their overriding responsibility to monitor the quality of all their organization does, and to see to it that it fulfills its agreed-upon mission. As a trustee, you are charged with keeping your institution on a prescribed and ever-enhancing focus which assures the long-term good of the organization.

It is an awesome undertaking. As a trustee, you have been chosen to be a guardian of the organization, and to demonstrate a dedicated concern for all of the constituencies you effect and touch. It is your job to protect the long-term interests of all who have a legitimate stake in the organization. As the guardian, as a trustee, you must ensure the success and the future well-being of your organization.

You nurture its traditions and heritage, you are a keeper of the vision, you are guardian of all that happens. It is your responsibility to guarantee the institution's future.

In doing all this, you walk a very tight line. Governing is not managing. Don't confuse the two. You are chosen to see that your institution is well managed, not to manage it.

68

CONTINUITY COUNTS

FOR AN INSTITUTION, THE continuity of trustees can be extremely important. Having an institutional memory has great significance. In some organizations, the learning curve can be complex and long.

Take a hospital, for instance. To be a conscientious trustee requires a great deal of reading, learning, and orientation. Peter Drucker says that being a hospital trustee is the most difficult position in any organizational structure. You don't learn a great deal the first year or two. In fact, it is reported that it takes a new hospital trustee several years simply to find their way to the hospital boardroom.

What is the optimum tenure for a trustee?

Ah, the toughest question of all. Everyone seems to have their own feeling about this and the answer probably is it really depends on the culture of the organization and the heritage of the board. My own strong feeling on the issue is that you start with the premise that: You never really let a good member get away.

But then, how do you retire trustees that aren't so good, that aren't that effective, that don't meet the major criteria of being a productive board member? That's difficult and there is no room for sentimentality. Just remember that shortly after mating, the black widow spider eats her mate.

If trustees don't attend meetings, it's easy. You let them know that you are certain they have great interest in the organization, but their time simply does not allow them to function as a trustee. You give them an opportunity to resign, and failing that—you nudge them into proper action. Remember the black widow spider. As a last resort, you may have to ask them to leave. This happens, and it can be done with a certain grace that permits the trustee to leave and still feel quite good about the organization. But you must take action of some sort. What value is a trustee who does not attend?

If a trustee has passing attendance but has not been really helpful in developing and enhancing the work of the organization—accept the fact that you have made a mistake. Just don't re-elect them. The Committee on Trusteeship should evaluate the work and effectiveness of each trustee before they are considered for re-election.

I am against life membership for a board member, but I am strongly in favor of Emeritus status. For the latter, an Emeritus trustee can return if they choose, but without vote. That is a very special way to release an important trustee position, but still keep a valued retiring board member within the loop. I have seen some boards work very effectively that have a number of Emeritus members. Those who care greatly about the institution continue to come regularly to board meetings and their opinions are solicited.

I know of several situations where Life Membership has been granted to trustees of special distinction. In the case of one, there are several founders of the institution who have

Life designation. The problem is, they continue to come to meetings and participate fully in the discussions. Their ardor and commitment for the organization is as deep and hallowed as it ever was—but their understanding of today's concerns and problems tends to be shallow. This type of a person can dominate a meeting and it is not pleasant to have to take a strongly opposite position with one whose roots are so deep—even though the memories and solutions are often from a time past.

I believe in the concept of six-on, one-off. Two three-year terms, and then off for a year. Some prefer three-year terms and one off, but I feel that can be too long. I go back to my original premise, however, that it depends so much on the culture and heritage of the board.

The key is to make certain that in the one year that an extremely strong and helpful trustee is off, they are kept totally involved and active—on a major committee, part of an advisory board, a member of the executive's inner circle, or whatever. It should be made clear that this is only a sabbatical, and you are expecting them to return. You don't want to lose them, and you certainly don't want them running off to another organization. You keep a stranglehold on them by having them remain active.

BEWARE THE LETTERHEAD-TRUSTEE

THE OTHER DAY, I spoke to one of the most important leaders of a major city. He told me he pretty much makes it a practice to accept membership on a board of a nonprofit whenever he is asked.

"But I tell them right up front—I'm not going to come to meetings and I'm not going to give. If you want my name on your stationery and for whatever other value it might have, I am willing to become a director."

I don't believe that kind of a trustee brings anything to the party. I seriously question the value of a letterhead-trustee.

In one community, we interviewed a half a dozen of the top leaders. They served on an advisory board of a very fine theater group in Spokane, Washington. Most of the leaders I talked with didn't even know that they were on an advisory board and in the case of one, he said: "Oh I guess I remember that someone asked if I would be willing to give my name. They promised that there wouldn't be anything for me to do. I'd forgotten all about it."

Some organizations may feel that it adds luster to have a very prestigious person identified with the organization, even if the involvement is negligible or non-existent. I have not known a situation yet where this has been helpful.

Some might argue that if you keep a person on your board, even though they might not participate—if you remain persistent, some day they may come through. I have never known this to happen, not in all of my experience. As one person told me: "With that group, I feel like I'm being nibbled to death by ducks. But I told them when they asked that I wasn't going to do anything, and I'm not."

Far too often an institution greatly overvalues the importance and effectiveness of having a letterhead trustee identified with the group. You can ill afford many of this kind. Greatness, in the end, can be measured only in the amount of devotion and dedication a person brings to their trusteeship. Honor and puffery count for little.

I remember when Lee H. Bristol, Jr., received an honorary degree from Hamilton College in New York. Lee was a graduate as was his father before him. A dozen Bristols have been identified with the institution.

During the graduation ceremony, and the conferring of the honorary degree, the President was quite effusive in his comments about Lee—deserved, but overflowing!

After the ceremony when Lee and his wife were walking across the campus, Lee said: "Louise, how many great people, really great people, do you feel there are in this world?"

"One fewer than you think, dear," said Louise, rather smugly, I thought, and without missing a beat.

70

BE OPEN
TO CHANGE

IN *PROCEEDINGS,* THE MAGAZINE of the Naval Institute, Frank Koch writes: "Two battleships assigned to the training squadron have been at sea on maneuvers in heavy weather for several days. I was serving on the lead battle-ship and was on watch as night fell. The visibility was poor with patchy fog, so the captain remained with me on the bridge keeping an eye on all activities.

Shortly after dark, the lookout on the wing of the bridge reported, "Light, bearing on the starboard bow."

"Is it steady or moving astern?" called the captain. Lookout replied, "Steady, captain," which meant we were on a dangerous collision course with that ship.

The captain then bellowed to the signalman, "Signal that ship: We are on a collision course, advise you change course 20 degrees." Back came a signal from the ship, "Ad-visable for you to change course 20 degrees."

The captain said, "Send this signal: 'I am a captain, change course 20 degrees.' "

"I'm a seaman second class," came the reply. "You had better change course 20 degrees."

By this time, the captain was furious. He spat out, "Son, I'm a battleship. Change your course 20 degrees."

Back came the flashing light, "I'm a lighthouse."

We changed course.

In a world that cries out for help in meeting urgent social agendas and human concerns, your board may need to change direction. Your constituencies seek help in finding solutions. You may have to change your course.

In today's world, your organization doesn't have the time or the luxury to stand by. You have this great moment of possible achievement, on the very razor's edge of opportunity. It is time for audacious action. Go for it. Seize the opportunity. If instead your board spends all of its time reviewing the minutes of the last meeting and revising policy statements, nothing will ever be attempted or achieved.

"There are no easy victories," says John Gardner. Group action can be agonizing, at times excruciatingly so. Group decisions are not easy, especially on matters of controversy or new direction. Proper funding can always be a problem. Now comes the real test. What is required of trustees is a strengthening of resolution, a rededication of commitment, and boundless faith. Even a willingness to accept Theodore Roosevelt's challenge: "To fail while daring greatly."

You must bring to each board meeting a probing, challenging, open mind. What are we achieving? Are we meeting our mission? What are our dreams and visions for the future? Is this the time to change our direction?

Understand that no matter how great and distinguished your past, your institution's most glorious victories are in the future. If you don't believe that, your organization is moribund.

The Do Do is extinct. A flightless, graceless, lumbering bird. Its ludicrous appearance gave form to the Portuguese word for fool—dou do. I've been told that the foolish Do Do flew backwards because it was more interested in where it was than where it was going.

Boards that worry too much about the loss of tradition or maintaining tired, out-dated programs, may well watch over the demise of something less than it might have been. Worry instead about the creation of something magnificent and marvelous. You should not suffer easily anything that is trivial, dull, or stagnant. A pretty bland diet, this sort of thing. Pablum!

No pain, no gain. No attempt, no triumph. No disappointment, no achievement. No cross, no crown.

71

DO IT

C ATHERINE QUINN IS IN her early 60s. Perhaps a bit older, but I wouldn't dare venture a guess. I do know for certain that she is as young in spirit as anyone I have ever met.

Catherine is a devoted member of the board of St. John's Hospital and its nursing home in Lowell, Massachusetts.

She doesn't need any public recognition. Everyone in the area knows and has great esteem for Catherine. And she doesn't need her name on another letterhead. There has been plenty of that.

She gives an immense amount of time to the work of the institution. And a great deal of money, also.

"I love that place and I care greatly about the things they are doing. It is an important part of my life."

Catherine points out, also, that one of the very special and added benefits of serving on the St. John's board is the close relationship she enjoys with other trustees. "You know, there's no other way I would have gotten to know some of these people with the depth that I have if it had not been for the board. I really look forward to the meetings because I enjoy these people so much. That's an added bonus of being a trustee."

I have a principle which is both wise and irrefutable. It should govern every action of every board. Here's the rule: You will be hurt more by those who would have said 'yes' who were not asked—than by those who say 'no.' Count on it.

Working together, ordinary trustees can perform extraordinary feats. A combination of all of their talents, linked together in a common and great cause—that can achieve miracles.

There is a whole world of men and women waiting to be asked, miracle workers just like Catherine Quinn. Go ahead, ask.

72

HOW MANY COMMITTEES?

DR. JAMES M. HARDY is one of the nation's foremost authorities on board and organization structure, governance, and trusteeship. Some may be as knowledgeable on the subject, but none are better.

He is known as Bo. He wouldn't know how to answer to anything else. Bo has written a half a dozen books on trusteeship. I have listed most in the bibliography. His latest is the best of the group and one of the best ever written on board structure.

In one of the sections, he writes about the number of committees that are needed in a typical organization, and he comes down on the side that claims "the fewer the better." A lot of experts concur with Bo.

I respectfully disagree. I believe that an organization should have as many committees as it needs. No more. But I opt on the side of more, rather than fewer. I'll explain.

And yes, I know, I know. God so loved the world, that he did not send a committee! Yes, yes I know. The camel is a horse, put together by a committee. Yes, a committee takes minutes, and wastes hours. There are a dozen more, but I shall spare you and go on.

If it is true, and it is, that some of the most important functions of board membership are the determination of policy, the giving or influencing of funds, and advocacy— then the case for a comprehensive committee structure is valid and emphatic.

All of the experience we have attests to the phenomenon that the more people are involved and the more they have an opportunity to participate—the greater they love you and the more they give. You've seen it yourself a hundred times. A man or woman on the board or in a committee meeting has an opportunity to take part in the discussion, they debate the issue before taking a vote, and all of a sudden it becomes part of them. There is ownership. And with ownership, you get commitment. It's bringing a trustee or committee member inside the institutional loop.

I feel that the more committees you have, the better it is.

But I suggest some corollaries with this concept. Each committee must be staffed. Therefore, the number of your committees may be limited by the number of staff you have. You don't want your chief executive officer spending all of his or her time attending meetings.

Trustees should serve on no more than two committees, three at the most. But that's the very most. Take the opportunity to bring non-board members into the organization by asking them to serve on committees. It's a significant way to broaden your leadership base and at the same time provide a feeder-sysem for future trustees. When an outside person serves on a committee and demonstrates the proper level of enthusiasm and commitment, good attendance, and strong participation—you have the making of a truly good trustee for the future.

What I am suggesting allows you to both abandon yourself and share in the strengths of others. It allows you to multiply the major leadership of the organization by a factor of four or five. It adds expertise, talent, and advocacy in a way that you could not possibly have by using only board members.

The strong and expanded committee structure also provides a platform for a very thorough and extensive discussion of any major issue or problem. In a committee forum, where a complex matter might be the only item that is reviewed and evaluated, concerns can be brought to the surface and constructively discussed. This is far more productive than having problems suppressed or ignored.

You will want to design a committee structure which is uniquely your own, totally appropriate to your needs. Let me suggest:

Executive
Finance
Investment
Property & Maintenance
Committee on Trusteeship
Program & Services
Personnel
Public Relations
Strategic Planning
Development

You'll want to add others that are just right for you, or eliminate some from this list.

Take the Public Relations Committee as an example. Two or three of your trustees will be extremely helpful and knowledgeable members for this committee. But then, I would add men and women in the area, not on your board, who have significant expertise—a couple of senior people from PR firms, the public relations director from a utility or a corporation, a business type whose PR antennae are always quivering. You get the idea. All of a sudden, you have a dozen people, only a few who are board members, who can help you plan and implement an exquisite and exciting program of public relations. Together and combined, these members will provide a soaring sense of high expectations and achievement for the organization.

There's more. I am a strong advocate of regular meetings—probably six or nine a year for most committees. This requires a good bit of staff time but I assure you, the dividends and yield are great. The planning of the agenda must be choreographed like a premier ballet, but it's worth it.

Something is wrong in an organization when efficiency conquers enthusiasm, bottom line wins out over service, and numbers become more important than the mission of your institution. This can't happen when you have the kind of dynamic and expanded committee structure I propose. Not if it is planned and staffed properly. You are on your way to a time of great achievement. I promise you.

You can measure the effectiveness and vitality of an organization by evaluating the commitment, energy, and advocacy of the trustees and the total committee structure. One follows the other.

You've heard about the fallacy, called "Post hoc ergo propter hoc." It means the rooster crows and the sun rises—therefore the crowing causes the sun to rise. That's nonsense, of course, but I promise you with the kind of full committee structure I recommend, the sun will shine brilliantly on your organization. As sure as day follows night.

73

LET'S HEAR IT FOR THE NON-REPRESENTATIVE BOARD

AROUND THE 1970s, THERE was a concerted and dramatic determination to move board membership toward a representative basis. The representative concept was and continues to be prevalent in the human and social agencies and organizations, more so than in other nonprofits. No more of the 'old boy' stuff. No longer the roster that reads like an exclusive club.

A representative board—the concept sounds good and it certainly provides for a more democratic structure. The problem is, with the representative board you may not be able to fulfill completely one of the most significant elements of trusteeship: To assure the proper funding and the ability to give or influence large gifts. That doesn't mean that this can't happen with the representative board—it's just more difficult.

We were involved recently with one of the ten largest

YMCAs in the nation. It was one of the largest—but it also had one of the poorest records of raising funds. Its board was comprised of an equal number of representatives from each of its twelve branches. The meetings were dull, mostly program reports. Worst of all, the board didn't have the muscle or even the will to make necessary determinations —decisions that impact the future of the organization and are of monumental value and consequence.

We recommended that the board, as it was constituted, become an Association Program Council and that a new group of men and women be enlisted—a blue ribbon group of the prime influentials in the community. This was done and great things happened. This group, by the way, brought as much energy and devotion to their task as all of those branch people had. Perhaps even more.

Some agency boards believe it is important to have pro-portionate representation of races and ages and an equal mix of all the constituencies served. Such a board would certainly be able to make intelligent and sensitive policy de-cisions. They would also bring to the board strong advo-cacy and meet many other trustee criteria. But that may not be enough.

There is a risk that such a board could not provide effec-tively for the proper funding of the organization. I've seen it happen.

A representative board can include so many different factions that it may turn out to satisfy no one. The danger is you may wind up with spirited discussions and a wonder-ful mix—and no funds. Be careful here.

There's a whole world out there of influential and af-fluential men and women, an army who cares greatly about your program and cause. And you can be certain that they will do more and more for you as you begin involving them in your board and committee structure. Don't penalize them by not inviting them to join your board and share in your cause—just because they may have influence and affluence.

74

THE E FACTOR

H E BELIEVES HE CAN do anything, and he incites all trustees in the excitement of it all. The pace is both exhilarating and exhausting.

I'm referring to James W. McLamore, co-founder and former chairman of the Burger King Corporation. He was able to use his ample entrepreneurial skills to build a new board of trustees at the University of Miami—considered one of the most powerful boards in higher education. McLamore and his trustees, together they took on audacious goals for the University. They call him "Mr. Miami." His influence and enthusiasm brought together an extraordinary group of volunteers. Miami had never before seen anything like it.

He considers himself a professional volunteer for worthy causes. "I hurl myself into my philanthropic activities." And 'hurl' is the operative word! He was elected to the

University board in 1973, was elevated to the executive committee in 1976, and became its Chair four years later.

McLamore decided to combine his chairmanship of the board with the Chair of the proposed capital campaign. This isn't often done or recommended. For the University, it really worked. But there aren't many like James McLamore. Everyone speaks about his energy and vision. He is one of those who fills a room with his presence.

He says: "Make no little plans." And he's never been found guilty of this kind of a problem!

He leads by example, as a good board Chair should. He personally pledged the first $1 million gift, and solicited all the other trustees to do the same. That 55-member board gave over $50 million to the campaign—about ten percent of the total raised so far.

When you ask anyone what his greatest gift is, they don't talk about the money or even his leadership. "Jim brings unbounded enthusiasm. It's contagious. We are all affected with it."

Beethoven once wrote: "From the glow of enthusiasm, I let the melody escape. I pursue it. Breathless, I catch up with it. It flies again. It disappears. I catch it again. I seize it. I embrace it. I delight in it. And at last, I triumph. And that is all there is to writing a symphony, and it all starts from the first glow of enthusiasm."

It takes enthusiasm. Board members must bring what I refer to as "a passion for the cause." Nothing less will do. Martha Ingram says that what she hopes for in a trustee is such great enthusiasm that it's not unlike a convert giving testimony at a revival meeting. A trustee must demonstrate abiding commitment and dedication, and raging enthusiasm—as John Quincy Adams once described it "from opening prayers through closing benediction."

75

HOW BIG A BOARD

THE MIRIAM HOSPITAL IN Providence, Rhode Island, has a board of sixty men and women. "It's not always easy to control a group of that size," says Edwin A. Jaffe, former Chair of the board.

That could be the governance understatement of the year.

When I ask Ed why so many members, he is quite clear that it has been structured for fundraising purposes. Does it work? "We raise more money than any other hospital and almost all other organizations in Providence."

But where's the control, how do you get anything done? How do you manage the operation properly? "We're the only hospital in the whole state that has a balanced budget. And we have been doing this for the past several years."

I'm certainly not recommending that large a board. For The Miriam Hospital, it seems to work. They also have an extremely active executive committee. This group meets often and discusses issues thoroughly so that major items can be brought to the board.

I asked Ed if this type of a model tended to take some of the decision-making power and incentive away from the board and give them the feeling that they were actually rubber-stamping decisions of the executive committee. "Yes, I think there may be that kind of a feeling and it's true. But they all come to the board meetings, there's a lot of enthusiasm for what we are doing, and there is a tremendous amount of loyalty for the hospital."

By the way, The Miriam Hospital just completed a successful campaign. It raised more than $9 million. This is the most that has ever been raised in the state for a healthcare institution. And the trustees played the major role in the program.

So what is the rule about size. There is none. The board should be only as large as is most effective for the organization. No larger. No smaller.

A few years ago at Scripps Memorial Hospital in La Jolla, California, there were thirty-six trustees on the board. And they were all really fine people and greatly interested in the work of the hospital. The problem was that with the kind of dramatic changes that were taking place in the healthcare environment, particularly in that area, there was some question as to whether a board that large could make the kind of decisions necessary to keep Scripps in the forefront of the marketplace.

They went from the large board to a seven-member group. These were folks who could meet often and had the talent and capacity to make quick decisions with wisdom and correctness. That's the kind of board Scripps needed most. And to this very day, this magnificent institution, one of the greatest community hospitals in the nation, functions with a lean board.

The large board, however, enhances your potential for raising funds. There can be no question about that. Bring the proper group of men and women together in a board setting, and noble action can transpire.

Laurence Tisch provides evidence that interest leads to involvement, and involvement to investment. There is proof-positive that the more a person is involved, the more they love your institution—and the more they love you, the more they give.

Tisch is the heavily media'd head of CBS, and a man of great resources. He devotes an enormous amount of time and money to his hobby—philanthropy.

Tisch is a trustee of the United Jewish Appeal and one of their largest donors. He is Chairman of the board of New York University and recently gave it $30 million for its Medical Center. He is on the board of the Metropolitan Museum of Art. It received $10 million.

Money follows commitment. Commitment is a result of involvement. You can count on it. You can take it to the bank!

Scripps Memorial Hospitals does have a Foundation, also—with over thirty of the most prestigious men and women in the community. This is the group that is charged with the raising and investing of funds. And what a high-flying group this is. They are well on their way to exceeding their $100 million goal for capital and endowment.

In *Governing Boards,* Cyril O. Houle writes that as far as size is concerned, "A board should be small to act as a deliberative body and large enough to carry the necessary responsibilities." But that doesn't help a lot. What's the rule about size?

The rule is: there is no rule!

76

STAMP LICKERS THEY AREN'T

THE OTHER DAY, I picked up a copy of Richard Cornuelle's powerful volume, *Reclaiming the American Dream*. For anyone interested in trusteeship and volunteerism, it is no more than one hour of exciting reading. Cornuelle invented the term: The Private Sector. And in this book, he makes the term come alive.

I didn't list the book in the bibliography because it was printed in 1965. I was concerned about the undue stress and frustration that would be caused by an army of people, all at the same time, seeking a copy. In case you have a streak of persistence, find the volume. It was published by Random House. It is a bright and immensely readable book, filled with high hope and soaring aspirations.

In one chapter, Cornuelle tells about a friend of his in San Francisco, a bright young attorney. The lawyer is with a prestigious firm, works extremely hard, and is rising rapidly in the profession. He will be a partner someday soon.

He has a deep sense of community obligation and takes on just about anything he is asked to do. He has joined several boards, and considers it an honor.

But what is he asked to do as a trustee? He sells Christmas trees on a frigid lot during the holidays. He begs for money from his friends, and doesn't like it very much. He sits through tedious board and committee meetings, where nothing significant happens, and even less is decided on. The meetings drone on—much is discussed about nothing. There is no sense of achievement, no feeling at all about the consequence of the organization's work.

Cornuelle says this is an example of a special talent, wasted. The board takes up chores and discussions a child could do as well. Too often, it is what one frustrated trustee reported to me: meetings of the unwilling, deciding the unnecessary, at the behest of the uncaring.

There is a whole world of people just waiting for the right cause. They are one with Jonas Salk who says: "I feel that the greatest reward for doing—is the opportunity to do more."

Trustees want significant work, and problems to solve that are of consequence. They are willing to become a board member because they feel that through their efforts, they can change lives and save lives. That is what propels them to a cause.

There awaits an energy explosion, ready to be unleashed. An army of men and women, just waiting to be asked.

I have found trustees willing to take on awesome responsibilities, if asked and properly motivated. They are willing to have someone keep raising the bar for them, and they'll keep jumping higher and higher. There is a tremendous potential, but often reduced to a trickle, forced through a narrow institutional funnel. Trustees need to see the results and consequence of their effort. They keep crying out: "Use me or lose me."

When given difficult and even time-consuming assignments, but projects that are important—trustees respond. One delightful surprise follows another.

Your board can do great things, waiting for the appropriate charge and challenge. Right now, there is the spirit and the heart to do great things, a quiet revolution ready to take place.

"Reverence for life," said Albert Schweitzer, "demands from all that they should sacrifice a portion of their own lives for others." No more Christmas trees and licking stamps for your trustees. Let's change the world.

77

SEVEN SINS OF TRUSTEESHIP

ONE DAY, SPEAKING TO a gathering of thousands, Mahatma Gandhi warned his people of what he called *The Seven Sins of the World.*

Wealth without work. Pleasure without conscience. Knowledge without character. Commerce without morality. Science without humanity. Worship without sacrifice. Politics without principle.

I have a list to suggest, more appropriate and relevant for the board member—*The Seven Sins of Trusteeship.*

- Acceptance without commitment
- Membership without attendance
- Affiliation without dedication
- Meetings without participation
- Decisions without integrity
- Involvement without advocacy
- Identification without giving

78

WHERE TO MEET

THIS MAY SEEM FAIRLY basic but anyone who understands group dynamics will appreciate the fact that certain settings lend themselves to a much more productive and participatory meeting.

A classroom setting, for instance, has the danger of a one-way interchange—from the Chair to the group. Effective and lively discussion is extremely difficult in this kind of a seating arrangement.

What works best is a T or a U configuration. The rule is: Do everything you possibly can to make certain that all board members have easy access and view to all others. A room with one long table doesn't work, and in some ways is even worse than the classroom setting. Even an oval table does not allow for perfect viewing. Typically, a circular table does.

One other interesting note, but of absolutely no significance. Have you ever noticed that even without markers or name cards, trustees invariably sit at precisely the same place that they did at the prior meeting, and the meeting before that, and the meeting before that? Even with boards that meet only annually, trustees will sit precisely at the same location they did at the last meeting. It has something mystical to do with the concept of territorial imperative and is not unlike the migration of birds. Once at a meeting of a hospital board, there was close to verbal abuse from one senior trustee who found his "regular chair" unconsciously and inadvertently taken by a new board member. It was not pleasant to behold.

In one small Indiana college, trustees complained about the total lack of discussion and the fact that their sessions were boring. They were meeting in a huge room, fifteen of them sitting around an immense oval table. The table was so large, they each had to have a microphone to be heard. It was impossible. No wonder there was little discussion. The setting was group-frigid.

The next quarterly meeting, we moved the board into a small but attractive room in the college library. They were almost cramped. But sitting around a circular table, small enough that they could touch, the session was lively, invigorating. There was question after question. They were energized. The setting made the difference.

It may seem like a small matter, but it does make a big difference. The physical setting and arrangements can help determine the vitality and participation at your meeting.

SEVEN DEADLY
POSITIONS

F AR TOO OFTEN, THE whole board seems to be apathetic. But no one cares!

When trustees get together, there should be an explosion of ideas. A board session should be the crossroads of success and towering growth, a meeting place of insatiable zeal and enthusiasm.

In my thirty years of being a consultant to philanthropy, I have attended hundreds and hundreds of board meetings —surely a sufficient number to earn me a place in heaven close to the martyrs.

Time and time again, I have heard the same seven deadly statements. You have, too.

We've never done it that way before.

Be willing to take a chance. Seize the opportunity. Some decisions require audacious action. It is impossible to consistently be both bold and infallible. For this decade, and into the new century, there almost certainly will not be a time without grave problems and great complexity. A board that protects its time-vested interests and its precious heritage—blocks necessary change. The result can be, at best, stagnation. At worst, paralysis extremis. The board member who is a hero is one who is filled with passionate intensity and in constant opposition to the status quo.

It can't be done.

In today's world, with the speed and constancy of change, to say 'impossible' always places you on the losing side. 'It can be done' must be your credo. An organization with an 'it can't be done' attitude will never be able to respond to human and social needs. Trustees must bring a dedication sufficiently resilient that they can pursue opportunities with vigor and fervor, despite any possible problems and potential setbacks. Trustees must be of heroic spirit and optimism. If you believe it can be done—it can be.

It will cost too much.

If the proposed program meets the mission of the organization, no cost is too high. If it truly affects the lives of those you serve, funds must be found. If the proposed activity provides an impact in extraordinary proportions, you must move forward. Trustees have convenantial responsibility to seek and provide the funds necessary to carry forward the mission and objectives of the organizations.

Not having funds is only a temporary problem, to be surrounded by creative solutions. To say you have insufficient funds for objectives that are of consequence represent trustee-manacles forged of rigid minds and lowly aspirations. You and other trustees have the final responsibility for proper funding—and that is a commitment to be taken with unrelenting resolve and intrepid dedication.

We're doing all right without it.

It was Will Rogers who said: "Even if you are on the right track, you will get run over if you just sit there." You can be certain that what is good enough today will not be adequate tomorrow. The changes that take place, almost from day to day, are profound and far-reaching. The mind can hardly fathom all the implications.

A great organization must have a sense of destiny and objectives which test its institutional mettle. Trustees must be willing to stand on tiptoes to reach out boldly, and there must be a willingness of heart and a courage of spirit that knows no bounds.

Too often, the attitude and focus of an institution that feels it is doing all right without change—is in serious trouble, and more difficult to change than a graveyard. And that is where it will soon be—dying for lack of creative nourishment. Those who are satisfied with today's progress and pace will unquestionably fall behind. The deterioration has begun and is well in place—because of the board's apathy, rigidity, and morale starvation.

Let's put it off for now and discuss it at a later time.

For a board, action counts. The decision seems to be quite clear. The matter has been reviewed by the appropriate committee, and approved by the executive committee. It is now time to make a decision. But someone moves that the action be postponed until the next board meeting so that there can be further review and evaluation. I call this analysis paralysis.

The chief executive officer of American Airlines says that clearly in 70 percent of the situations where a decision is required, it really doesn't matter whether the board votes yea or nea. Either decision could be correct. What kills the organization is not making the decision at all. It is quite clear, there isn't a solution to every problem. Very often, what really makes the difference is a response of some sort. Action!

To postpone a decision is in effect, to make one. This is perhaps a time when healthy impatience has great virtue. Indecision is contagious, and its effect casts an unhealthy pall over each member of the board. Analysis paralysis, in the end, causes organizational atrophy. Ross Perot says that too often, an organization says: 'Ready, Aim,

Aim, Aim, Aim.' What Perot *recommends instead is the concept of: 'Ready, Fire, Aim.' The theory is valid. Most often, it is far better to take action, even though all the factors may not be totally clear, than to take no action at all. If all possible objections must first be over-come, nothing will ever be attempted.*

We've tried it that way, and it didn't work.

Try again! Try again and again. Every problem is an inspiring opportunity when pursued with a vigorous belief in the possible. Trustees must always consider 'what might be'—and not be shackled by 'what is' or what happened in the past.

The right idea is a dream put into action. The wayside is filled with organizations that started with great vision and zeal, but lacked the stamina and fortitude to finish. Their places are taken by institu-tions with trustees with ideas, trustees who never know when to quit. There is a compelling inner force and an irrepressible drive to succeed —to break their own records, to outstrip their yesterday by today, and to do their work with more resolve and dedication than ever before.

To forge ahead, that's the mightiest force of all. Words and dreams are overabundant, but ideas that rouse can change the world.

We're not ready now.

If not now—when? Today, this is the day of unconquerable opportu-nities. Never have demanding expectations been higher and needs greater. Never has everything been in such perfect position to achieve such re-markable results. Today is the day to seize the opportunity! This is no time to deny or abdicate. It would be a serious failure of heart and spirit. A decaying of moral fortitude, determination, and courage.

Now, now is the time. You must move forward and your decision must be forged by the smithy of hard work, persistence, and commit-ment.

Pray for a miracle, but work for results. Board and committee meetings do not necessarily move mountains. Bulldozers do.

If not now—when? There can be only one response. Now!

IT TAKES
COURAGE

I T'S NOT EASY. AT times, it takes courage and a willingness
to dare the impossible.

When the Dean of Seville assembled his parishioners in
the Court of the Elms, he admonished them: "Let us build
a church so great that those who come after us may think
us mad to have attempted it."

And beyond courage, it requires resolve—a never-ending
doggedness and determination to see it through. Churchill
said: "Never give up. Never, Never, Never, Never."

I challenge you to dedicate yourself to the mission of
your institution, and to pursue with a missionary's zeal the
quality which makes you premier in your service.

I challenge you to demonstrate a willingness to dare, ex-
plore, to break through old barriers, and to reach out for
new horizons.

I challenge you to condemn all in your organization that
is dull, grim, and without motion or risk.

History will deal kindly with you if you are willing to take a position, and throw your heart and spirit into the terror, the surprise, and the exhilaration of the unexplored.

IT'S NOT HOW IT BEGAN

It didn't start out this way.

When I first had thoughts about writing a book on governance and trusteeship, I wanted to develop a theme that was focused entirely on the need for trustees to give and raise funds. That was my primary concern and theme.

I have nearly fifty books on governance in my library. To my dismay, I found only a few provide any substance to the importance of trusteeship involvement in the proper funding of an institution. To my way of thinking, having the appropriate financial resources to meet an organization's mission should be one of the most urgent imperatives that concerns a trustee. I still feel this is true.

But something very special happened in the development of this book. I interviewed a number of men and women I believe are really effective trustees. There were about a hundred in my group. From all over the country. These were magnificent people, these trustee leaders.

I believe that in my career, I have worked and met with over a thousand different boards—and I have served as a trustee of a half dozen institutions. But in all my work, I had never really studied what motivated trustees to give the kind of time and energy that is required to be a proper steward of the institution. I had never even dug very deep to determine why they gave funds, more than ever when they became trustees.

And that is what actually started me on this extraordinary and fascinating journey, an exploration of the truths and principles that govern trusteeship. Much of what I heard is quite similar to what Jacqueline Grennan Wexler reports. She is the former Roman Catholic nun who was president of Hunter College in New York, and just recently retired as president of the National Conference of Christians and Jews. Read what she says: "Well, I hope I take seriously that to whom much has been given, much will be expected. I believe that what we have been given is diverse, that each of us has different gifts to invest...

"I have only one life and so many hours and so many dollars to invest, and I want to invest my time, my relatively limited financial resources, and my experience in places that can make a difference...and I try to make time for that."

I heard virtually the same type of comment from every person I interviewed. There is the sense of paying back, what many referred to as: "paying the rent."

They told me how greatly they valued their trustee experience and the immense joy they feel in giving to others. Many echoed what one university trustee told me: "I feel that in my own way, I am helping to make a great difference in the world. I give a lot of my time and talent to the school and by doing this, I am certain that there are some young people whose lives have been changed because of what I have been able to do." That's it. I heard it time and time again—the fact that trustees are helping to change lives and save lives.

And yes, of course, I heard a great deal about raising funds and making gifts. Not one I spoke with backed away from this. All understand that "the giving and getting" function of their trusteeship is a responsibility which cannot be abdicated.

I was overwhelmed with the concern, care, and compassion that was demonstrated by trustees. I was impressed, also, with the great joy and delight they spoke of in their stewardship. It seemed to me that in all of my fifty volumes on governance, I learned a great deal about the principles, process, and techniques of governance—but precious little about the joy and passion. But it was there, with every trustee interviewed, in great abundance.

I wanted this book to be more than practice and process. I wanted to express the dedication and devotion that trustees feel. I wanted this book to be a celebration of trusteeship.

Initially, when I first conceived of the book, I thought of it being written for mostly the staff—chief executives and senior fundraising staff. But then, I reviewed my shelf of fifty books again and realized that virtually all were written for the staff. Oh certainly, there are a number of fine ones that are just as relevant for those men and women who chair their boards. But even more significantly, the books tended to deal mostly with the policies and practices that govern board structure and organization. There was virtually nothing of what I refer to now as the passion and dedication that is so integral a part of trusteeship. That's what was missing. And that is what has led me to the type of book I have written.

I've included much about method, procedures, and standard practices. But these are mostly surrounded and embraced by the spirit and heart of trusteeship which I found in such extraordinary proportions. That is the thread that is woven throughout the book.

I have a feeling that trustees who read this volume, and particularly those who have been board members for some time, may well say to themselves: "I could have written this very book." I believe that this may be the mark of a book of some considerable common sense. I am pleased! It puts into words your own thoughts and perhaps, in some small way, adds insights and guidelines you had not yet discovered.

It's extraordinary—the virture, wisdom, and judgment that trustees bring in such monumental increments to their organizations and institutions. The numbers boggle the mind: there are boards in 500,000 churches, 4,000 hospitals and medical centers, 3,000 colleges and universities, and over 400,000 social and human service agencies. And foundations, museums, and libraries. The list goes on.

Men and women from all over the country—they commit selflessly of their time, energy, talent, and money. There appears to be no limit to the extent they are willing to give of their dedication and devotion. This glorious army of men and women, their passion knows no bounds.

These trustees, they bring ingenuity, spirit, and hope— and they combine that with an unlimited source of time and energy. They bring it all together with the American impulse of vigor and enterprise, a mounting agenda of zeal and mission. With Susan B. Anthony, their credo is: Failure is impossible.

These trustees I interviewed, they have a genius for solving problems, some very complex. And the few I talked with are only a minute sampling of the millions and millions who all over the country serve and provide the great voice for social responsibility and determine the reshaping of the human agenda. They speak loudly, these trustees.

Ah, the American experiment is alive and well.

No other nation in all the world can match our concept and structure of trusteeship. Certainly, there are a few countries that follow our model, but none that brings the vigor and dedication we do to the task.

It's a mysterious thing. At times, almost magical. It's hard to know what makes it all happen, what brings it together, and why it seems to work so well.

All you know is that you are part of something truly significant and it's worth all of the time and energy you have given it. There isn't even time to ask: "Who the devil talked me into all of this?"

Trustees somehow bring together a magnificent combination of good deeds and indeed doing good. They do not do well as spectators. They believe that people who stand still and watch from the sidelines of life, find only a partial existence. They die without having lived. They come to the end, never having experienced life.

These wonderful men and women, these trustees, they give shape and form to our organizations. They nurture all things that represent quality and excellence. They are repulsed by shoddy, pedestrian, and ill-defined programs.

We celebrate trusteeship because it gives witness to an institution's strength, character, audacity, and vitality. John Lewis Russell best expresses it when he says: "It is one of the glorious celebrations of this life that no one can help another without helping himself."

This book does indeed celebrate trusteeship. It is not dedicated to those who have served on boards in the past, although that group is indeed worthy of acclaim. It is dedicated instead to present trustees and for all men and women who follow. The cup is passed to them. It is an awesome responsibility they take on, and an audacious venture. To them, the charge—to maintain, in a constant state of renewal and revitalization, the American dream.

HOW TO MEASURE BOARD PERFORMANCE

THE FOLLOWING EVALUATION (CALLED Trustee Assessment of the Board—TAB) is designed to permit board members to take stock of the board's over-all performance and compare it to the performance of other boards. TAB allows you to measure your board against characteristics and criteria that are generally accepted to be important in rating board effectiveness.

As you will note, TAB is a fast-paced evaluation that only takes a few minutes to complete. The questions it raises may lead you to suggest procedures or approaches that can make a difference in performance or attitude.

If your organization is not performing as well as it should, chances are good that this will be reflected in board performance. Weak board, weak institution—the two almost always go together. On the other hand, the stronger the performance of the board, the greater the likelihood your institution will be serving at a peak level. One thing is certain: there is a direct relationship between your work as a trustee and the service your institution provides.

The Trustee Assessment of the Board is custom designed for trustee enhancement and growth. It has been field-tested. The evaluation instrument and the Trustee Assessment of the Board matrix are copyrighted. We want you to use this information as often as you want. Please feel free to copy it. We ask only that you credit it in the following manner—Source: *Boardroom Verities* by Jerold Panas.

TRUSTEE ASSESSMENT

CRITERIA AND CHARACTERISTICS	Score Rating
1. Quality of participation at board meetings	
2. Chair's encouragement of trustee participation	
3. Time provided the chief executive officer to give status reports	
4. Manner in which the agenda is planned in advance to assure coverage of important items	
5. Priority given to major and long-range issues versus day-to-day matters	
6. Material and information sent in advance of board meetings to prepare trustees	
7. Extent to which trustees do their pre-board meeting homework	
8. Attendance at board meetings	
9. In terms of the institutions needs, the number of times the board meets	
10. In terms of the institutions needs, the size of the board	
11. Board's working relationship with the chief executive officer	
12. The board's working relationship with the administrative staff	
13. Trustee's practice of not interfering in functions reserved for administration	
14. Speed with which minutes are mailed following a board meeting	
15. Board's knowledge of major committee activity	

OF THE BOARD—TAB

5	3	2	-1	-2	0	0
Very Good	Good	Fair	Poor	Do Not Have	Not Applicable	Not Certain

TRUSTEE ASSESSMENT

CRITERIA AND CHARACTERISTICS	*Score*
	Rating
16. Regularity with which the board conducts a self-evaluation	
17. Process for selecting new trustees	
18. Process for electing board officers	
19. Regularity of meetings by the board's standing Committee on Trusteeship	
20. Regularity of annual audits and financial report presentations	
21. Quality of financial reports	
22. Opportunity for discussion following financial report presentations	
23. Amount of time given to discuss committee reports	
24. Trustee commitment to making gifts to the institution	
25. Willingness of trustees to solicit gifts from others	
26. Trustee commitment to ensuring an adequately funded institution	
27. Quality of planning for board's annual retreat	
28. Attendance of trustees at the board's annual retreat	
29. Board's attention to the investment of reserves and endowment funds	
30. Orientation of new board members	

OF THE BOARD—TAB

5	3	2	-1	-2	0	0
Very Good	Good	Fair	Poor	Do Not Have	Not Applicable	Not Certain

TRUSTEE ASSESSMENT

CRITERIA AND CHARACTERISTICS	Score Rating
31. Board evaluation of the chief executive's work	
32. Salary structure for the chief officer and staff compared to others in the field	
33. Practice of reviewing and revising the mission statement of the institution	
34. Camaraderie and esprit of the board	
35. Tendency of trustees to act as a team	
36. Degree to which the institution's short-term objectives and long range goals are understood by trustees	
37. Board's practice of monitoring the progress of its objectives and goals	
38. Board's concern for the institution's success in serving its client-constituencies	
39. Board's concern for the institution's success against its competition	
40. Board's practice of trustee rotation and tenure	
41. Recognition of retiring trustees	
42. Board's use of staff people to make reports at meetings	
43. Board's use of client-constituencies to make presentations at meetings	
44. Regularity of trustee inspection of the institution's facility and departments	
45. Board's enforcement of policy prohibiting conflict of interest with trustees and their business relationships	

OF THE BOARD—TAB

5	3	2	-1	-2	0	0
Very Good	Good	Fair	Poor	Do Not Have	Not Applicable	Not Certain

TRUSTEE ASSESSMENT

CRITERIA AND CHARACTERISTICS	Score Rating
46. Level of trustee involvement and work	
47. Degree to which trustees consider this board affiliation their primary volunteer involvement	
48. Trustee willingness to support policy	
49. Effectiveness of standing committees	
50. Regularity with which governing policies, by-laws and the like are reviewed for relevancy	
51. Mix of the board (age, interest, business affiliation, past experience, financial resources, and so forth)	
52. Quality of information provided trustees to interpret the work of the institution	
53. Board's attention to the institution's public relations	
54. Board's attention to the allocation of funds	
55. Board's focus on generating gifts rather than reducing expenses	
56. Board's sense of fiscal responsibility	
57. Degree of opportunity to discuss information before making important decisions	
58. Openness of board meetings	
59. Extent to which board meetings offer information about the institution's work	
60. The overall effectiveness of the board	

OF THE BOARD—TAB

5	3	2	-1	-2	0	0
Very Good	Good	Fair	Poor	Do Not Have	Not Applicable	Not Certain

SCORING

1. Number rated *Very Good:* _____ × 5 = _____

2. Number rated *Good:* _____ × 3 = _____

3. Number rated *Fair:* _____ × 2 = _____

4. **TOTAL** _____

5. Number rated *Poor:* _____ × (minus) -1 = _____

6. Number rated *Do Not Have:* _____ × (minus) -2 = _____

7. **TOTAL** _____

Subtract line #7 from line #4

8. #4 = _____

9. minus #7 = _____

10. **TOTAL NET SCORE** _____

11. Number of *Criteria and Characteristics in Grid:* 60

12. Number marked *Not Applicable* or *Not Certain* _____

Subtract line #12 from line #11 _____

13. Number of items you checked for tabulation _____

To determine average, divide line #10 by line #13

14. Total Net Score (#10) _____

15. Divide by Checked Items (#13) _____

16. **YOUR AVERAGE SCORE IS** _____

RANKING

4 and above	A Superb board. Your institution is assured of growth, development, and success. You are headed for greatness.
3 to 3.9	An Outstanding board. But take care of those few areas where you are deficient.
2 to 2.9	A Good board. Review carefully those areas that need correcting. With proper attention, you could be outstanding.
1.4 to 1.9	You are not functioning as well as you should. Appoint a Special Task Force to evaluate your practices and implement necessary changes.
1.3 and lower	You have problems that should be corrected. Chances are almost certain that your poor showing reflects, also, the performance of the institution. Improve your effectiveness and the institution is assured of improvement.

BIBLIOGRAPHY

I have listed here only books that I feel are particularly helpful and significant. A few have only an indirect impact on board membership and governance, but each in its way can make a consequential contribution to your tenure as a trustee.

Abbott, Charles C. A GUIDE FOR TRUSTEES AND DIRECTORS. The Cheswick Center, 1979.

Alexander, John O. PLANNING AND MANAGEMENT IN NONPROFIT ORGANIZATIONS. THE NON-PROFIT ORGANIZATION HANDBOOK. Editor, Tracy D. Connors. McGraw-Hill, 1980.

Anthes, Earl; Jerry Cronin and Michael Jackson. NON-PROFIT BOARD BOOK: STRATEGIES FOR ORGANIZATIONAL SUCCESS. West Memphis, Arkansas: Independent Community Consultants, 1985.

250 pages. Available for $24.50 plus $2.50 shipping from Independent Community Consultants, Post Office Box 1673, West Memphis, Arkansas 72301.

Anthony, Robert N. and Regina Herzlinger. MANAGEMENT CONTROL IN NONPROFIT ORGANIZATIONS. Richard D. Irwin, Inc., 1975.

Axelrod, Nancy R. THE CHIEF EXECUTIVE'S ROLE IN DEVELOPING THE NONPROFIT BOARD. National Center for Nonprofit Boards, 1988.

Bader, Barry S.; Richard J. Umbdenstock and Winifred M. Hageman. BOARD SELF-EVALUATION MANUAL. Rockville, Maryland: Bader & Associates, Inc., 1988. 145 pages. Available for $110 from Bader & Associates, Inc., Department 100, Post Office Box 2106, Rockville, Maryland 20852.

Barry, Bryan W. STRATEGIC PLANNING WORKBOOK FOR NONPROFIT ORGANIZATIONS. St. Paul, Minnesota: Amherst H. Wilder Foundation, 1986. 85 pages. Available for $25 plus $1 shipping from Management Support Services, Amherst H. Wilder Foundation, 919 Lafond Avenue, St. Paul, Minnesota 55104.

Baughman, James C. TRUSTEES, TRUSTEESHIP, AND THE PUBLIC GOOD: ISSUES OF ACCOUNTABILITY FOR HOSPITALS, MUSEUMS, UNIVERSITIES, AND LIBRARIES. Westport, Connecticut: Quorum Books, 1987. 187 pages. Available for $35 plus $2 shipping from Greenwood Press, 88 Post Road West, Westport, Connecticut 06881.

Carver, John. BOARDS THAT MAKE A DIFFERENCE: A NEW DESIGN FOR LEADERSHIP IN NON-PROFIT AND PUBLIC ORGANIZATIONS.

1990, 242 pages. The Jossey-Bass Non-Profit Sector Series.

Collins, Judith and Barbara Von Elm. WHAT LIES AHEAD—A NEW LOOK. United Way of America, 1983.

Conrad, William R. and William E. Glenn. EFFECTIVE VOLUNTARY BOARD OF DIRECTORS: WHAT IT IS AND HOW IT WORKS. Athens, Ohio: Swallow Press, 1983. 244 pages. Available for $9.95 plus $1.85 shipping from Voluntary Management Press, Box 9170, Downers Grove, Illinois 60515.

Dayton, Kenneth N. GOVERNANCE IS GOVERN-ANCE. Washington, D.C.: *Independent Sector,* September 1987. 14 pages. Available for $3 from *Independent Sector,* 1828 L. Street, N.W., Washington, D.C. 20036.

Drucker, Peter F. MANAGING THE NONPROFIT OR-GANIZATION: PRINCIPLES AND PRACTICES. 1990, Harper Collins Publishers, 235 pages.

Duca, Diane J. NONPROFIT BOARDS; A PRACTICE GUIDE TO ROLES, RESPONSIBILITIES, AND PERFORMANCE. Phoenix, Arizona: Aryx Press, 1986. 228 pages. Available for $28.50 from Oryx Press, 2214 North Central at Encanto, Phoenix, Arizona 85004.

Fisher, James L. THE BOARD AND THE PRESIDENT The American Council on Education, MacMillan Publishing Company, New York, 1991. 163 pages including an index and extensive bibliography.

Fram, Eugene H. NONPROFIT BOARDS: THEY'RE

GOING CORPORATE. *Board Leadership and Governance.* The Society for Nonprofit Organizations, 1989.

Fram, Eugene H. and Vicki Brown. POLICY VS. PAPER CLIPS: SELLING THE CORPORATE MODEL TO YOUR NONPROFIT BOARD. Milwaukee, Wisconsin: Family Service America, 1988. 146 pages. Available for $12.95 plus $2 shipping from Family Service America, 11700 W. Lake Park Drive, Milwaukee, Wisconsin 53224.

Frantzreb, Arthur C. NON-PROFIT ORGANIZATION INDIVIDUAL GOVERNING BOARD AUDIT. McLean, Virginia: Arthur Frantzreb, Inc., 1988. 7 pages. Available for $2 from Arthur C. Frantzreb, Inc., 6233 Kellogg Drive, McLean, Virginia 22101.

Gardner, John W. ON LEADERSHIP. The Free Press, New York, 1990.

Girl Scouts of the USA. GIRL SCOUT COUNCIL SELF EVALUATION. New York: No. 26-175, 1982.

Hardy, James M. CORPORATE PLANNING FOR NONPROFIT ORGANIZATIONS. Association Press, 1972.

Hardy, James M. THE CORPORATE BOARD IN A VOLUNTARY ORGANIZATION. JMH Associates, Erwin, Tennessee: 1984.

Hardy, James M. DEVELOPING DYNAMIC BOARDS. Essex Press, Erwin, Tennessee, 194 pages, including extensive bibliography and extremely useful Appendix of grids and forms.

Hardy, James M. MANAGING FOR IMPACT IN

NONPROFIT ORGANIZATIONS. Essex Press, Erwin, Tennessee, 238 pages.

Herman, Robert D. and Heimovics, Ricard D. EXECUTIVE LEADERSHIP IN NONPROFIT ORGANIZATIONS: NEW STRATEGIES FOR SHAPING EXECUTIVE-BOARD DYNAMICS. Jossey-Bass Inc., Publishers, San Francisco.

Herman, Robert D. and Jon Van Til. NONPROFIT BOARDS OF DIRECTORS: ANALYSES AND APPLICATIONS. Transaction Publishers, 1989. 203 pages. Available for $29.95 plus $1.40 shipping from Transaction Books, Rutgers University, New Brunswick, New Jersey 08903.

Houle, Cyril O. GOVERNING BOARDS: THEIR NATURE AND NURTURE. San Francisco, California: Jossey-Bass Publishers, 1989. 225 pages. Available for $19.95 plus $1.95 shipping from the National Center for Nonprofit Boards, 1225 19th Street, N.W., Suite 340, Washington, D.C. 20036.

Howe, Fisher. THE BOARD MEMBER'S GUIDE TO FUNDRAISING. Jossey-Bass, Inc., Publishers, 1991, 180 pages.

Ingram, Richard T. TEN BASIC RESPONSIBILITIES OF NONPROFIT BOARDS. National Center for Nonprofit Boards, Washington, D.C., 1988. 22-page booklet.

Ingram, Richard T. and Associates. MAKING TRUSTEESHIP WORK: A GUIDE TO GOVERNING BOARD ORGANIZATION, POLICIES AND PRACTICES. Washington, D.C.: Association of Governing Boards of Universities and Colleges, 1988. 184 pages. Available for $19.95 (members), $23.95 (nonmembers) from the Association of Governing Boards of Universities and Colleges, One Dupont Circle, Washington, D.C. 20036.

Johnson, Everett A. and Johnson, Richard L. CONTEMPORARY HOSPITAL TRUSTEESHIP. Teach'em, Inc., 1975, 198 pages.

Lord, James Gregory, THE RAISING OF MONEY: THIRTY-FIVE ESSENTIALS EVERY TRUSTEE SHOULD KNOW. Cleveland, Ohio: Third Sector Press, 1983. 128 pages. Available for $34.50 from Third Sector Press, 2000 Euclic Avenue, Post Office Box 18044, Cleveland, Ohio 44118.

Nason, John W. FOUNDATION TRUSTEESHIP: SERVICE IN THE PUBLIC INTEREST. New York, New York: 1989. 186 pages. Available for $19.95 plus $2 shiping from The Foundation Center, 79 Fifth Avenue, New York, New York 10003.

Nason, John. NATURE OF TRUSTEESHIP. Washington, D.C.: Association of Governing Boards of Universities and Colleges, 1982. 136 pages. Available for $15.95 (members), $21.95 (nonmembers) from the Association of Governing Boards of Universities and Colleges, One Dupont Circle, Washington, D.C. 20036.

O'Connell, Brian. AMERICA'S VOLUNTARY SPIRIT. A BOOK OF READINGS. 459 pages. The Foundation Center, New York, 1983.

O'Connell, Brian. THE BOARD MEMBER'S BOOK: MAKING A DIFFERENCE IN VOLUNTARY ORGANIZATIONS. New York, New York: Foundation Center, 1985. 208 pages. Available for $16.95 from The

Foundation Center, 79 Fifth Avenue, New York, New York 10003.

Pocock, J.W. FUNDRAISING LEADERSHIP: A GUIDE FOR COLLEGE AND UNIVERSITY BOARDS, 1989, The Association of Governing Boards of Universities and Colleges (One Dupont Circle, Washington, D.C. 20036), 151 pages.

Seltzer, Michael. SECURING YOUR ORGANIZATION'S FUTURE: A COMPLETE GUIDE TO FUNDRAISING STRATEGIES. New York, New York: Foundation Center, 1987. 514 pages. Available for $19.95 plus $2 shipping from The Foundation Center, 79 Fifth Avenue, New York, New York 10003.

Swason, Andrew. BUILDING A BETTER BOARD. The Taft Group, 1984.

United Way of America. CITIZEN BOARD IN VOLUNTARY AGENCIES. Alexandria, Virginia: United Way of American, 1979. 75 pages. Available for $2.50 from United Way of America, 703 North Fairfax Street, Alexandria, Virginia 22314.

Umbdenstock, Richard J.; Winifred M. Hageman and Barry S. Bader. IMPROVING AND EVALUATING BOARD PERFORMANCE: THE COMPLETE GUIDE TO SELF-EVALUATION OF THE HOSPITAL GOVERNING BOARD. Rockville, Maryland: Bader & Associates, Inc., 1986. 84 pages. Available for $12 from Bader & Associates Inc., Department 100, Post Office Box 2106, Rockville, Maryland 20852.

Young, Donald R. and Wilbert E. Moore. TRUSTEESHIP AND THE MANAGEMENT OF FOUNDATIONS. Publisher: Russell Sage, 1969.

Index

About the Author

Jerold Panas is executive partner of Jerold Panas, Young & Partners, Inc.—one of the nation's largest firms specializing in campaign services and financial resource development. In addition to *Boardroom Verities,* he is the author of three best-selling books: *Mega Gifts, Born to Raise,* and the *Official Fundraising Almanac.* The National Society of Fund Raising Executives selected *Mega Gifts* as one of the 25 most outstanding books published in the fundraising field.

Mr. Panas is the founder of Decision Research Institute, one of the leading market research firms in the nonprofit field. He is chairman of the board of the Institute for Charitable Giving—a national group that provides seminars for professionals and board members in the nonprofit field. He is also chair of the National Healthcare Board, which publishes health letters for hospitals.

His principal office is at 500 North Michigan Avenue, Chicago, Illinois 60611 (312-222-1212). Other offices are located in San Francisco, Atlanta, Sidney, and Melbourne.

Other Books by Jerold Panas

Mega Gifts
Who Gives Them, Who Gets Them

This book helps you understand and put to work the motivations and incentives behind large gifts. Selected as one of the 25 most important books on fundraising by the National Society of Fund Raising Executives.
$34.95. ISBN 0-931028-39-6. Hardcover.

Born to Raise
What Makes a Great Fundraiser

Here are 50 interviews with fundraisers who tell what it takes to be the best. This first-ever study of fundraising skills discloses controversial and surprising conclusions and suggestions.
$34.95. ISBN 0-944496-02-4. Hardcover.

Official Fundraising Almanac

This extraordinary volume of resource and reference material has been called an enormous contribution to the field. It brings together information that makes fundraising more effective and productive—and a little easier.
$39.95. ISBN 0-944496-07-5. Paperback.

Published by

Precept Press, Inc.
160 E. Illinois St.
Chicago, IL 60611